De Grazia
the irreverent angel

PHOTO BY LOUISE L. SERPA

De Grazia
the irreverent angel

by William Reed

Frontier Heritage Press 1971 San Diego, California

Contents

Foreword by
Dr. Harold McCracken

Ted De Grazia is an extraordinary individual, and his art is as extraordinary as the modest man who creates the winsome impressionistic angels and ceremonious Indians of the Southwest, for which he has become internationally famous. His style is so nearly unique that it defies imitation.

Significantly, De Grazia and his work are the product of an era in which the basic values of good art and beauty have severely been challenged or destroyed in the minds of many by attempts to find new ways of artistic expression. This unfortunate trend was brought about by a faction of radical artists, who have called themselves the *avant-garde*. They have undertaken to predominate the whole art scene, from classrooms to museums, with not-good abstractions, pop-art, illegitimate sculpture, and other wild adventures into the bizarre and absurd. But it has become increasingly evident, among collectors and in the marketplaces, that these experiments have accomplished little more than frustration, both in and out of the fields of academic art. Now there is a strong trend back to the traditional.

De Grazia is not a follower of any academic school or trend in art. Instead, he has

created something that is quite new and pleasantly refreshing. For he is at heart a maverick—which Mr. Webster defines as "an unbranded range animal" or "an independent individual who refuses to conform to his group." The quiet charm and beauty of this artist's impressionistic paintings of Indians and angels presents a contrast to the artless products of the *avant-garde* that is as remote as anything in art could be.

I have known Ted De Grazia and observed his work for a number of years. The ultimate goal he is reaching, is not the result of the college degrees in art and music, nor the academic training he has had; nor has the sophistication he has gained as a distinguished artist to any degree spoiled him for the close association and friendship he has enjoyed with the Indians he portrays. I have been with him when we visited his friends the very primitive Seri Indians in the deep back country of Old Mexico; and I have been with him in the homes of his Yaqui friends on fiesta night. There is no mistaking the complete compatibility in the relationship. They call it *simpático* in the Latin countries. From observing the friendship that De Grazia has with the natives he portrays, it is easily understood how he puts such a depth of sympathetic feeling into the beautiful paintings he creates around these people. It could not otherwise be.

Never before has there been a wider popular interest in art, or a larger number of more active collectors and patrons, than there are today. This is particularly true of the "Western" field, both past and contemporary. Many are the neophyte artists who have

THREE CHILDREN

been undertaking to become followers of Remington, Russell, and Bierstadt. And there is no reason why the new Western art cannot follow the best of the traditional good craftsmanship, beauty, and dignity. Mediocrity never long survives. And more people than ever before are seeking the truth as to what is really *good* art, and what is *not* so good. They are also trying to determine who among the contemporaries are most worthy of collecting, and may survive to be considered great in the future. As to this no one really knows. Only one thing is certain, and that is that time and time alone will be the final judge. A proper and lasting evaluation of art has been tormenting even the best of critics for centuries. They have not even been able to agree on a definition for great art—for art, in its finest form, is a many splendored intangible. What one judge may prefer, another may not. Nevertheless, there are certain basic characteristics to be found in the works of most great artists. Good craftsmanship and consistent quality are fundamental; as is also a quality of strongly appealing in a pleasant way to a large number of discriminating people. Probably the most definite hallmark of a great artist is a distinctiveness that sets that artist's work apart from all others. For example, a Remington or a Childe Hassam or an Andrew Wyeth can be identified about as far away as they can be seen. These qualities certainly are to be found in the magnificent work of Ted De Grazia. In the opinion of this writer he is foremost among the American impressionists.

YAQUI DEER DANCER
Cast Bronze, Height: 72"

The Seri Know

*To see the world in a grain of
  sand,
And a heaven in a wild flower;
Hold infinity in the palm of your
  hand,
And eternity in an hour.*

WILLIAM BLAKE

A quiet morning darkness hung over the Seri Indian village of Desemboque, Mexico. In the east, the first faint trace of light framed a semi-circle of desert and mountain. To the west, the ocean lay cloaked in blackness, its presence confirmed only by the gentle lap of waters along the shore below.

From the village came the crow of a cock, joined some moments later by a chorus from near and far. There was a stirring of movement in the campsite, and a man arose slowly, swung his feet to the ground, and sat silently on the edge of his cot, staring seaward. He was joined some time later by a younger companion. The man on the cot raised a hand as the other approached and said, "Listen!" From the seashore below came a rhythmic thumping, as of a drum beat. "You hear that?," asked the man seated. "That's a signal from one of the Indians in those boats there along the shore. He's calling his crew members, telling them the tide is right. The sea turtle are waiting, and it's time to start the hunt." The other man sat down on the edge of the cot, and nothing more was said for some time. The sky lightened, and the two men watched the scene unfold along the shore.

The amorphous outline of the village now began to separate itself into individual dwellings, among which one could see the scurrying figures of women preparing the morning meal. The men moved more slowly, making deliberate preparation of equipment to be used on the hunt. The drumming continued, and now it was possible to see the man in the boat thumping on the inner bottom planking with the blunt end of his long fishing spear. Now also, one could hear the chatter of happy voices and the laughter of children.

The older man ran his hand thoughtfully through the white hair of his beard and whistled softly to himself. This was an old and familiar scene. For some years now he had traveled among the scattered villages of the

PHOTO BY VINCENT MEIR

Seri—sketching, painting and observing with practiced eye the tenor of their lives. To the Seri he was known as "the bearded one." They were not surprised at his coming; less surprised at his going. He was not a *turista*. They accepted him—this strange one—as he accepted them.

Later in the morning the Indian women came. They carried with them their items of barter—long strings of shell and bone beads, handsomely woven baskets, and polished ironwood carvings. From chattering groups, the bolder ones pushed forward to display their handiwork. The more reticent retired to the edge of the camp and spread their wares over brightly colored cloths on the ground. Dirty faced, ill-clothed or naked children hung at their mothers' skirts, while half-starved dogs sniffed and prowled through the belongings of the newcomers. The harsh light of day brought into sharp focus the primitive reality which night had softly covered over. As the sun rose higher, its rays beat down upon the decaying seaweed, burnt

SERI FISHERMEN, oil, 8″ × 12″

turtle shells, and vegetation along the shore; an overpowering stench rolled in waves over the camp and surrounding area. It was impossible to ignore, yet the Bearded One seemed oblivious to the dirt and squalor. A group of laughing Seri women strolled along the beach toward the upper end of the village. They saw that he was watching and turned quickly away, some covering their faces with their hair. "Beautiful," he murmered, "beautiful."

By this time the two other men of the party had arisen. Soon the smell of wood smoke and frying bacon helped to cover the odor from along the shore. Over breakfast, the four men watched in silence as a cool breeze to seaward gently dissipated a low-lying fog bank and revealed the mountain tops of Tiburon Island in the distance. The older man pointed toward the Island. "That's where these people belong. Once it was theirs. Do you know the legend?"

Without waiting for an answer, he continued.

"According to the Seri, a giant leather-back turtle arose from the sea in ages past and gave birth to the Seri people. The turtle became the Island of Tiburon—mother, father, protector, and home of the Seri. Some years back, the Mexican government moved the Seri here to the mainland and established

SERI COOKING THE TURTLE, oil, 14" x 20"

Tiburon as a game preserve.

"It was the beginning of the end."

He waved a hand in exasperation.

"Look around you! Only a handful of the Seri cling to their heritage. It's a damned shame. Soon they will become 'civilized' like us."

There was silence for a moment. The man walked to the campfire and poured himself a cup of coffee. He turned suddenly and pointed toward the village. "Look at that hut over there! Just bent ocotillo branches covered with brush, but notice the color and the form! The Seris have been living in such homes for centuries. Tough? Hell yes!, it's been tough, but they have used that toughness as a whetstone. Maybe that's what's wrong with us; we're losing our whetstone." He pulled at his beard, and stared to seaward. "I can't help but notice that most of the Seri still know how to laugh spontaneously; their emotions are natural, not conditioned like ours. They envy us for what we have; I envy them for what they are."

The Bearded One walked back to the cot and sat down, holding his head in his hands. After a time he spoke, as if to himself. "You know, it's very important to be satisfied only with what you need. Maybe the Indian has the right philosophy: 'When you get your *olla* full, then you should stop working and enjoy its reward; then work again when it is empty.' I keep coming back down here. I don't know why. Maybe I'm looking for something I don't have. I'm not sure exactly what it is . . . but I think the Seri know."

On a rocky, desert hill some distance northeast of the city of Tucson, Arizona, stands a Gallery in the Sun. It does not intrude upon the face of the earth as a stranger. The adobe and cactus-spine and rock and wood elements of its construction are the natural elements of its environment. It is not a static monument to the cold technology of man, but rather a warm yet emphatic reaffirmation of one man's faith in the land which gave him birth and strength. The structure is an extension-in-character of the man who dreamed it and built it. He is a painter. There are those who point their finger and shake their heads. Unlike the Seri, they do not accept him. They call him eccentric, and bemoan the fact that he will not conform. He calls himself simply, De Grazia.

The following sketch is not a precise and detailed history of De Grazia's life; it is a literary portrait. It may be classed as a biography, but the story does not rest upon a chronological imperative. Quite simply, it attempts to interpret the relationship between the reality and the essence of a complex man in search of simplicity.

Mature simplicity is an art that does not come easily. It is the product of pain, experience, and a hard courage. Such things belong exclusively to those who have earned them. They belong to men like Ettore "Ted" De Grazia.

In a sense, this is his story. In a deeper sense, it is the story of every man who has refused to follow that path not of his own making.

BY THE SERI SEA, oil, 10" × 18"

Chapter One

*He who doubts from what he
sees
Will ne'er believe, do what you
please.
If the Sun and Moon should
doubt,
They'd immediately go out.*

WILLIAM BLAKE

It was a typical New York television interview show. The interviewer looked bored. "Maybe I've been at this too long," he thought. "These yahoos are all alike." He adjusted his chair while waiting for the "on-the-air" signal and threw a professional smile of encouragement toward the waiting interviewee. "Jesus!" he muttered to himself. "I wonder where they dug this one up? What was his name? Oh yeah! De Grazia. Southwest artist . . . paints Indians and angels. . . ." The interviewer almost laughed out loud. "That's a good one! Angels! This guy would probably do better painting devils. He looks like the Devil himself . . . and that garb!"

He took a closer look and shook his head in disbelief. "Somebody has to be kidding," he thought. ". . .a beard like Moses; well-worn cowboy hat; cowboy shirt, open at the neck and topped with a black cowboy neckerchief; faded western pants and scuffed cowboy boots . . . and what is that thing hanging from a strap over his shoulder? Looks like an Indian medicine bag." He wasn't sure why, but suddenly he felt himself getting angry.

De Grazia returned the stare, and the faintest hint of a smile danced briefly in the sparkle of his eye. He removed the battered western hat from his head with one hand and wiped beads of sweat from his forehead with the sleeve of his shirt. "Hot, ain't it?," he asked.

The interviewer nodded agreement. "Yeah, it sure is." To himself, he said, "And it's going to get hotter, cowboy."

Then, out of the corner of his eye, he saw the broadcast engineer raise a hand in warning. The signal light flashed on, and the interviewer smiled into the camera.

"Good evening, ladies and gentlemen. We are honored to have with us today a real live westerner from Arizona. He may look like a cowboy, or an Indian, but he's much more than that. He is, in fact, a southwestern artist of some renown—Mr. Ted De Grazia."

The interviewer turned to his "victim" with a demeanor of mock seriousness. "Mr. De Grazia, I understand you paint Indians and angels. I was wondering . . . do you do your research first hand?" He giggled.

"I mean, I can understand an Italian painting angels—even an Italian cowboy—but isn't it a bit unusual for an Italian to be such an expert on Indians?"

"Oh, I don't know," replied De Grazia. "Christopher Columbus did all right in that department, and we've had a lot of experience since then. As a matter of fact, I can't really consider myself an Italian, because I tend to live in the past. I prefer to think of myself as an Etruscan!" A few snickers were heard from the audience, and the interviewer laughed nervously.

"Well, be that as it may, isn't it true that you are primarily an abstract artist?"

8

DREAM HORSE

"I hate titles. Everybody wants to fit you into a nice, neat, predictable package. I'll tell you what . . . you call me what you like!"

"Well the thing I don't understand, Mr. De Grazia, is how you can hope to 'capture' the Indian in the abstract. Wouldn't the school of 'realistic' art be more suited to painting a valid historical picture? For example, how about Catlin, Miller, Remington, and Russell?"

"How about them?," countered De Grazia. "Do you expect me to say they weren't good? Damn right they were good. So are a lot of contemporary Western painters. We just happen to paint in a different language. Why do you insist on comparing us? A lot of people object to my art on the grounds that it isn't 'photographic.' Hell! I don't want it to be! They say, 'That horse's neck is too long,' or 'That saddle doesn't even have a cinch!'" He laughed. "Maybe they object to my purple bulls because they haven't seen one. Well, that doesn't really bother me."

"But I thought one of the strong points of Western art was the emphasis on historical and artifactual accuracy."

"For some people it is," said De Grazia. "Don't misunderstand me; I have nothing against realistic art . . . done a lot of it myself before I discovered the art that was really me. I guess it depends upon whether you're more interested in a piece of 'frozen' history, or a work of art that speaks in more than one language.

"What do you mean?"

"Well, take 'realistic,' for example. As the title for a school of art, I think that word is a misnomer. 'Realistic' art sure doesn't have much in common with realistic experience. You know, life is made up of more than ice cream colors and detail. It's a multiple experience of sight, sound, color, movement— these things generate emotions. Most of what we experience is more 'felt' than seen. Now, with the proper use of color, I can suggest these things to you through the abstract, but it's pretty hard to capture in a precise 'slice of life,' no matter how prettily painted. Don't you agree?"

"Yeah, I guess so," murmured the interviewer. He began to get the feeling that this "cowboy" might not be as easily handled as he had thought. He tried another approach.

"Mr. De Grazia, I understand that you are the most 'reproduced' living painter. Do you have any explanation as to why your paintings, cards, and prints sell so well, even during periods when other good painters are having a hard time making rent money?"

De Grazia pulled a rumpled, red handkerchief from his hip pocket and casually blew his nose.

"That's easy. I'm the best!"

MOTHER & CHILD BY YUCCA PLANT

PHOTO BY LOUISE L. SERPA

After his initial shock, the interviewer laughed to himself. That did it! He was surprised at the intensity of his anger, but he was determined to put this egotistical bastard in his place.

"Isn't that a bit immodest? I mean, your public must deserve some credit for your success. And, how about the art critics? Don't you think you owe them a little something for making you what you are today?"

"Art critics!" snorted De Grazia. I don't owe the art critics a damned thing! Actually, I'm not even sure what a 'critic' is. The few I've heard call themselves that are miserable bastards, feeding off someone else's talent.

"I'm only interested in people who buy my paintings because of an honest emotion. They buy my paintings because they sense something of what I am trying to say. My paintings are my life. They are my experience. They are what I have felt and known. Such things are not expressed easily in art. In the beginning it was an almost impossible thing. It is still difficult, but if I considered others when I painted, then it would be something not my own.

"I don't compare myself with another painter. When I paint, there is no other painter. People ask me, 'What is your best painting?' I tell them, 'The next one. I haven't painted it yet. I am in competition only with myself, and that's tough, because I believe that each thing I do must be better in some way than the last."

De Grazia paused, pulled a can of snuff from his "medicine bag," removed a pinch with his thumb and forefinger, and placed it carefully behind his lower lip. Fixing the interviewer with a meditative stare, he said: "I don't know why people get so upset when I say, 'I'm the best.' I wouldn't give a damn for a man who didn't believe in himself. I *have* to think I'm the best. Don't you?"

The remainder of the interview turned to safer ground.

The foregoing is a typical example of how De Grazia affects many people. His psychological makeup is a complex mingling of unbounded self confidence and a defensive facade of bizarre action and statement. This is a weapon which he wields with abandon when he feels challenged; it is used more subtly during his frequent moods of mischief. Those who know him well can tell the difference by the intensity of the gleam in his eye.

Perhaps this technique of defense is not an unusual characteristic for a sensitive soul born into the tough, mining-camp-world of Morenci, Arizona.

11

NAVAJO SQUAW

Chapter Two

There is a sacred horror about everything grand. It is easy to admire mediocrity and hills; but whatever is too lofty, a genius as well as a mountain, an assembly as well as a masterpiece, seen too near, is appalling.

VICTOR HUGO

For more than a hundred years, the desert mountains of Morenci have yielded up their treasure of copper ore. Never has it come as a gift. The treasure has been given under duress to a tough, determined, "no-nonsense" breed of hard-rock miners. It was into this challenging environment that Ettorino "Ted" De Grazia was born on June 14, 1909, the third of seven children born to Domenico De Grazia and Lucia Gagliardi De Grazia, both natives of Italy. As a boy, he grew up as lean and hard as the desert rocks among which he worked and played.

From the beginning, he was an enigma—a "loner." While other children played collective games, Ted often sat alone carving figures from the hard desert clay which, to his mother's dismay, he then insisted upon baking in her oven — usually while she was baking bread.

De Grazia recalls:

From childhood, I have been interested in color. To some people, Morenci looks harsh and barren. To me, it has always been a world of beauty and color. Often I would go on long hikes with my father, and we would fill our pockets with colored minerals. These rocks I crushed with a hammer for color. Color fascinated me. It made a deep impression which has persisted to this day. I treasure a head of Christ I modeled in native red clay, baked hard in my mother's oven.

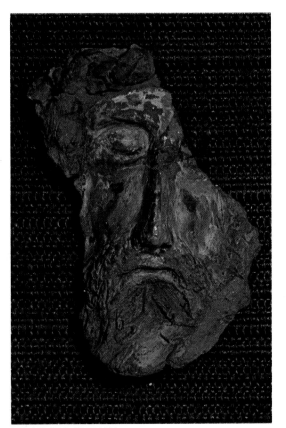

HEAD OF CHRIST
Natural clay, Height: 6"

De Grazia's artistic ability was apparent at an early age, but this was not a golden key to societal acceptance and praise. This was not Vienna; this was Morenci. Here life was tough and hard. There was no room for artistic nonsense and daydreaming. Survival depended upon pitting one's wits against the environment, not embracing it as a friend. The boy De Grazia never learned to accept this philosophy. For him, the desert was a thing of inestimable beauty; a flowing form of color, silent-sounds, and delicate movement. When the world of "You must do!" became too much, De Grazia retreated to the desert and into his own world of dreams. It was not a world of inactive dreams, but it was a world which had no place in Morenci, Arizona. It was here that the pattern was set for De Grazia the boy and De Grazia the man — sporadic forays into the harsh world of reality, but always the withdrawal into the unreal-reality of his own desert kingdom.

The only significant period in his life in which De Grazia was away from the desert came with the slowdown of work in the

14

Morenci, Arizona Territory, 1910

Morenci mines in the year 1920. His family moved back to Italy for an extended visit. It lasted five years.

"While there," De Grazia recalls, "I got a good education in Church art. I watched the Church decorators and artists and soon began to work with clay. Then I got some paints and tried to paint pictures, always with the religious theme. I still consider the church art of Italy to be some of the finest ever painted by man."

When the De Grazia family returned to Morenci from Italy in 1925, Ted had to learn to speak English all over again. Furthermore, he had to start over again in school, entering the first grade when he was sixteen years old. Seven years later, he graduated from Morenci High School at the age of twenty-three.

These years were spent not only on formal education in the classroom but, during the summers, on a more meaty education in the land which was to become his second home — Mexico. The majority of Morenci miners were comprised of immigrant laborers from the land below the border, and young Ted often traveled with them on their journeys to and from families left behind. As a result, he speaks Spanish like a *puro paisano*.

CHRIST ON THE CROSS
Cast bronze on wood, Height: 20"

Most of the Mexican miners came from the state of Chihuahua, the birthplace of the well known Mexican bandit — or patriot — Pancho Villa. So many came from Chihuahua, in fact, that legend records Morenci as the birthplace of the Mexican revolution led by that notorious leader. It was in Mexico — that incongruous land of pain and beauty — that Ted De Grazia absorbed — as only a boy can — much of the depth of understanding and feeling which characterize his paintings of the Mexican-Indian.

During the period following his return from Italy, De Grazia became seriously interested in painting. He still has in his possession paintings dating from 1925. At first, he sketched and painted the landscape and the conventional themes, but he discovered a whole new world of Mexican art when he picked up a brush and began to paint the Mexican miners of Morenci.

It is, of course, a futile exercise to speculate to what degree "chance" influences the course of a man's life, but perhaps in Ted De Grazia's case, music was of equal importance to art in deciding the trail that he ultimately chose to follow. You see, Ted De Grazia also played a mean trumpet.

After graduation from high school, De Grazia worked in the mines with his father, but with the shutdown in 1932, he decided to attend college. When he entered the University of Arizona in 1932, he had fifteen dollars in his pocket and a trumpet under his arm. The trumpet and a pick and shovel put him through college.

At first, he played in local groups, then with a band, and before long he had an orchestra of his own. Some indication of the merit of this musical group can be deduced from the realization that one of the performers in De Grazia's early orchestra was that legendary genius with a horn, Teddy Essex.

His musical background, coupled with the fact that at the university De Grazia also came under the influence of Professor Joseph De Luca of the College of Music — former assistant to John Philip Sousa—decided him on a career of music. It was an uncertain decision, however, for the restless De Grazia dropped out of school a few semester hours before receiving his bachelor's degree in music. This was prompted not only because of his inability to shake the influence of art, his first love, but also by the demands of economics — and the beat of the marital drum.

ALONE, oil, 10" × 18"

In 1936, De Grazia was married (officially) for the first time. Almost predictably, the marriage was as unusual as the man himself.

Since De Grazia is a Catholic, it was not unusual that he was married in St. Augustine's Cathedral in Tucson.

It was, however, perhaps a bit unconventional that the High Mass for the ceremony was sung by a friend who just happened to be a Jewish cantor.

Shortly after his marriage, De Grazia moved with his bride to a small border town in Arizona, where he managed a theatre of the family "chain." It didn't take him long to realize that the mundane world of business was not for him. Strange drives and impulses within him kept insisting on giving voice to the course of his life. He did not fully understand the language of their prompting, but he knew he must give attention to their demands.

Always, the voices led to Mexico.

By this time, De Grazia was long past the stage of *turista* in Mexico. He had become intimately acquainted not only with the residents of almost every small village and hamlet in the Mexican states of Chihuahua and Sonora, but of many places south as well. And, he continued to paint. No matter that his art was often criticized, misunderstood, and punished with social rejection. These were his adopted people, and he understood their love of the land, their simple emotions, laughter, sorrow and tragedy. He painted them in the only way he knew how — honestly.

There is little doubt that at this point in De Grazia's life, art exerted a major influence. But the trail was not yet chosen and mapped; it was, rather, a time of searching.

The searching led to extremes of fulfillment and extremes of disappointment, but it would not be silenced. Its paths were many and varied. During the following few years De Grazia was in and out of work, in and out of school, and in and out of marriage. No small part of his unhappy moments were prompted by the desire of his family that he pursue business, or a teaching career, as opposed to his own stubborn desire to follow the precarious path of the artist.

Acceptance came slowly, punctuated by long periods of indifference to his work, but De Grazia continued to paint. In his spare moments, he began to experiment with ceramics, mosaics, and silversmithing.

Occasionally there were moments of

PHOTO BY JACKIE SHARKEY

De Grazia and Yaqui Dancers

18 good fortune and encouragement, such as the following offering by Charles Tracy, eminent surrealist, author, dramatist, and artist:

Every once in a while nature plays odd tricks. She produces with monotonous regularity standard patterns, then as though in a humorous mood she surprises and often shocks us by turning out something that does not fit into our grooves . . . She produces children who know instinctively more than we can teach them . . . We cannot understand these odd ones . . . often we punish them with our social indifference or worse. Geniuses thus have a more difficult time getting recognition than those who perform as we expect them to. But . . . geniuses are not to be denied . . .

Mr. Tracy then went on to prove himself a very good prophet.

Ted De Grazia came to me only a few months ago with a half dozen attempts at paintings. I knew at once that regular art instruction was not for him; so I encouraged him . . . In these days we tag such painters as 'primitives.' I would indeed be surprised if Ted is not discovered as such and his works hanging in many museums of fine art within five years or less. Ted De Grazia understands and sympathizes with the underprivileged Mexicans and with bold direct brush strokes he paints as his heart directs . . . it is his kind of art and it is wonderful.

There was one other who, in the beginning era of De Grazia's art, believed in this young, eccentric artist.

Raymond Carlson, editor of *Arizona Highways* magazine, saw in the paintings of this "primitive" the seeds of greatness. In the February, 1941 issue of *Arizona Highways*, Carlson reflected upon a local De Grazia showing, "Dust of Mexico:"

The most learned comment we can make about De Grazia's work is that we would be very proud to own his painting 'Defeat,' because we like it very much for we, too, feel very deeply about Mexico and the simple people there and the painting makes one feel good inside . . . You should spend some time following the vagrant country roads that ramble about northern Sonora and learn to know and understand the people you meet along those roads. Then you'll like the paintings of Ted De Grazia.

"One would expect," comments De Grazia, "that after a plug like that you might hope to sell a few paintings. Actually, I did sell a few, but damned few. Those were pretty dark days, and more than once I considered throwing in the towel and going back into business. It was a constant struggle between the call of the artist and the demands of economics."

In 1942, the artist won; De Grazia packed his bags and set out for Mexico City. There, he worked with the renowned masters of Mexican art, José Clemente Orozco and Diego Rivera. Both men had a profound im-

pact upon the mind and art of the young De Grazia: "In college, the professor usually looks down upon you as a dumb bastard. It was not like that with Rivera and Orozco; they treated me as an equal. They made me feel — for the first time in my life — that maybe I was somebody after all.

"I worked on murals with both men; on the second-floor of the National Palace with Rivera, and with Orozco at the Hospital of Jesus in Mexico City. It was a good experience — and those were good days!"

Rivera and Orozco sponsored De Grazia in a one-man show in the Palacio de Bellas Artes in Mexico City in November, 1942. Their encouragement gave the young artist great hope.

Diego Rivera wrote:

. . . his paintings greatly interested me because of his brilliant artistic gift and his personal sentiment, so original that it prevails through some strange influence, perhaps unconscious. The fugue in the execution of his painting, his acute romantic and exalted observation and his feeling for proportion give the certainty that when developed as an artist, De Grazia will become a prominent personality in American art.

Orozco was even more emphatic in his prediction:

De Grazia's painting has all the freshness, simplicity and power of youth. He is able to go from the simple and graceful movement of the 'Cocks Fighting,' to the understanding of human misery as in the 'Boy Playing the Violin.' He will be one of the best American painters some day.

Sparked by the impetus of his Mexican conquest, De Grazia gathered up his brushes and paints and headed for Tucson, expecting the laurels of a returning Caesar.

It didn't work out quite as he had planned.

Galleries wouldn't show his work. The University of Arizona turned down the show that had been so successful for De Grazia in the Palace of Fine Arts in Mexico City. "Why?" De Grazia asked himself. "Why?"

The fact that he was ignored hurt him worse than the fact that he damned-near starved. Yet, even in the darkest moments there were moments when the sun shone through. De Grazia remembered the encouragement of Charles Tracy and Raymond Carlson; and there were others—not in sufficient numbers, unfortunately, to guarantee daily bread upon the table, but enough to sustain hope for the future.

In 1943, De Grazia "The Primitive" returned to the University of Arizona. Although his studies were sporadic, due to other commitments — such as work in a defense plant — he graduated with a master's degree in art in January, 1945. Along the way, he also picked up two bachelor's degrees, one in music and one in art.

De Grazia's master's thesis forms a backdrop to an understanding of his art today, for it speaks of his understanding and use of the dramatic color and form which instantly identifies a "De Grazia." De Grazia decided that he would title it: "ART AND ITS RELATION TO MUSIC IN MUSIC EDUCATION."

"I thought the idea was original," said De Grazia, "but I soon discovered that the same concept was first voiced over two thousand seven hundred years ago!"

WOMEN WITH BUNDLE ON HER HEAD

Chapter Three

Technique! The very word is
like the shriek
Of outraged Art. It is the idiot
name
Given to effort by those who are
too weak,
Too weary, or too dull to play
the game.
The mighty have no theory of
technique.

LEONARD BACON

Color has been a major preoccupation with De Grazia from the days of his boyhood in Morenci, where he crushed rocks and boiled or pounded the roots and foliage of desert plants in an attempt to extract natural pigments.

"Color," he affirms, "is a language that speaks to us by appealing to our emotions. I became obsessed with this idea as a boy, and off and on for years I experimented with various methods of expressing this concept in art. You know, some paintings have 'magic!' You know immediately when it happens. Occasionally, some of my paintings had this magic, but it was a phenomenon which I could not control at will. I was convinced that, for me, this magic came from an instinctive use of the right color with the right form, but I was frustrated because I couldn't find a logical explanation for it. This problem bothered me for years, and I kept coming back to it time and again."

Most of man's discoveries of great moment are the products of accident. So it was with De Grazia. It happened one day while he was painting to the background music of a radio symphony.

"I noticed," said De Grazia, "that as the tempo and timbre of the music changed from, for example, sombre to light melody, I tended to select colors in my paintings which suggested similar feelings in me. I got to thinking about the relationship between art and music, and for the first time it occurred to me that form in sculpture and painting is closely represented in music by rhythm and harmony. By the same token, color in art is tied in closely with melody and timbre in music . . . especially by modulation of the voices. This may have been a discovery of no great universal impact, but for me it was the beginning of a life-long study, and it has from that moment had great influence on my art."

In 1944, De Grazia was to develop this idea — the relationship of art and music — in his master's thesis. More importantly, in later years he carried it to fruition in his art, an accomplishment which has earned him international recognition as a master in the field of color. His ideas on the subject are well expressed in his thesis:

It is true that as we look at a painting that is a masterpiece of art which has survived through the ages, we find that what makes it great is not whether it is realistic or not, or because of its subject matter . . . its merit depends upon the play of light and color and the relationship of one form to

PHOTO BY DICK FRONTAIN

another, making a composition expressive and alive . . . In our own age especially, when the camera has surfeited us with realism and the true-to-life possibilities of painting have been adequately developed, we must turn to abstract painting in order to have more freedom in expressing in a crea-

FREE AS THE WIND, oil, 16" × 34"

tive way what we feel rather than what we see . . . a kind of painting that can suggest motion, speed, action.

Basically, music and painting are the same, the common root being emotion . . . probably *feeling* is a better word to use than emotion, since feeling means more . . . One thinks of feeling as referring to the whole of man.

"I was very surprised," De Grazia remembers, "to discover during research for my thesis that my ideas concerning music and art were certainly not original. Sometime before 322 B. C., Aristotle commented that, '. . . we find colors may mutually relate like musical concords for their pleasantest arrangements like those concords mutually proportion.' "

De Grazia further brings out in his thesis the fact that although Aristotle had the first recorded comment on the subject, Leonardo Da Vinci was probably the true founder of the modern art of abstract color. Da Vinci recognized the primary emotional characteristics aroused by colors centuries before the psychologist dreamed of the idea. This study has been carried on by a number of researchers over the centuries and, although they certainly do not all agree, the following tabulation is in general acceptance today:

Color	Characteristic	Symbolism
YELLOW	restless warm most luminous positive	pleasant cheerful
RED	exciting aggressive warm restless positive	rage danger courage virility
PURPLE	stately rich pompous impressive	nobility spirituality
VIOLET	cool retiring	color of a woman no longer fruitful
BLUE	cool serene passive retiring	sincerity hope serenity
GREEN	restful cool passive retiring	faith immortality resurrection
WHITE	positive stimulating	truth purity innocence chastity
MIDDLE GRAY	mellow richness	sedate sober old age
BLACK	depressing	sorrow gloom death fear

"Such charts," states De Grazia, "are today in general use in a number of modern art institutes. They are used as a function of technique. Although *generally* valid, they also constitute a definite danger and pitfall to the aspiring artist. Such techniques often encourage new painters to distrust their natural instincts and to depend upon a more scientific approach. This can take the life out of a painting.

"In other words," De Grazia continued, "A painter should have a thorough grounding in the psychology of color, but he should also be prepared to violate it if he is to tell his own story in his own way. With the proper instincts, a painter can use color effectively to prompt a desired emotional response in the viewer. In the same way, he may suggest ideas of movement, velocity, direction, and even mood, through use of the exaggerated or incomplete line in his construction.

"Most of what we absorb in life is on the periphery of our vision. We view life as a combination of color, sound and movement, seldom, if ever, 'frozen' for us into a precise

24

DESERT FANTASY, watercolor

and predictable image. In a sense, as I have said before, abstract art can be construed as perhaps the most realistic art of all. It attempts to interpret life as we realistically experience it—emotionally. One must be careful, however, to distinguish between abstract art that attempts to say something meaningful about something that is meaningful and an abstract art that turns inward upon itself. Too many painters today have forgotten the important lesson that true art is a form of life-interpretation, not merely an exercise in technique."

Some years after De Grazia received his master's degree, he met and spent some time with Thomas Hart Benton at Martha's Vineyard. Benton was impressed with De Grazia's style and use of color, and in a later article titled "Master of Fantasy," commented:

When so much artistic energy is absorbed, as it is today, in the search for fantastical correspondences in line, color, and shape, and when a fanciful inventiveness has become almost the sole motive for aesthetically directed performance, to be named master of fantasy would not seem to suggest any great distinction. However, there is a difference between an art of fantasy and a fantastical art. . . .

Little by little for the past hundred years . . . the artist has lost his purpose and art no more speaks of the thoughts and ideas of social man but only of itself—and, very largely, to itself. . . .

Very different is the fantasy of Ted De Grazia. He himself is as much an abstractionist as anybody but he manages to abstract *something* because his attention is directed to *something,* a something which exists outside himself and his special concerns with artistic procedure. . . . His painted world is an intangible one of iridescent floating colors but it calls up, and poignantly, that real world of the desert which he loves and close to which he lives.

The desert itself is like a fantasy, like something in a dream. Desert shapes are, of course, as solid as anywhere else and desert distances as measurable but they don't seem so . . . ordinary realistic perceptions are inadequate for catching the qualities of the desert vista. But De Grazia's fantasies, rapidly improvised as they appear, tenuous shimmering wisps of color as they are, do catch them and reveal them to us better, I think, than they have yet been revealed in painting. . . . We are much in need of an art like this. De Grazia has shown up at the right time.

But what of De Grazia's theory concerning the relationship of art and music? It was not enough, he suggested, that an abstract relationship be conclusively estab-

Thomas Hart Benton paints DeGrazia on a visit to Tucson

lished between the two; this had been done. De Grazia was obsessed with the idea of translating this theory into a practical instrument. Why not construct a musical instrument which would match musical chords with a visual color spectrum—so related as to prompt similar emotional response? Obviously a good idea, he discovered, because this too had been done. Over a period of hundreds of years, such experiments had been tried by many men. Isaac Newton had devised a prism color and scale; Erasmus Darwin had suggested the use of a light-on-color organ; Hermann von Helmholtz had experimented with spectral and pigment mixtures; Ewald Hering had developed a

GIRL WITH BROOM

theory of color-vision, and Alexander Scriabin had developed a workable machine to demonstrate the relation between color and music. There were others too: Goethe, Ostwald, Bertrand Castel, and Wallace Rimington, to name but a few. No matter, De Grazia would build his own device.

The result was a light-spectrum machine, with which De Grazia spent months translating into color the works of Tschaikovsky, Brahms, Stravinsky, Wagner, Beethoven, Sibelius, and Rachmaninoff. He proved to himself the workability of his idea and made a number of provocative suggestions in his thesis concerning the use of color-music techniques in the home, industry, church, and school. More importantly, he developed in the process a "feel" for color which began to express itself dramatically in his paintings. True, they still weren't selling like hotcakes, but he knew they were good. No matter that Aristotle had said it before . . . he could say it again, and better!

Faced with the fact that galleries still refused his work, and with a growing stack of paintings in the corner of his studio, De Grazia decided to take the bull by the horns.

Undaunted by the fact that he had no money, he decided to build himself a gallery!

"Why in the hell not?" he argued to himself, "I've certainly got something to put in it—I've got the world's largest collection of original 'De Grazia's!'"

STRAVINSKY'S SONG OF THE NIGHTINGALE, oil, 26" × 32"

Chapter Four

Art is a jealous mistress, and, if a man have a genius for painting, poetry, music, architecture, or philosophy, he makes a bad husband. . . .

RALPH WALDO EMERSON

De Grazia's first gallery, at Prince and Campbell streets in Tucson, is a monument to the complex-simplicity of the man himself. Simple in the adobe and wood and cactus-spine elements of its construction it is complex in the seemingly haphazard, but artistically pleasing arrangement of its many rooms, cubicles, outbuildings, and "Mexican-Villa"

decor. De Grazia made the adobe bricks himself and, with the help of Yaqui Indian friends, accomplished the heavy labor of construction as well.

Money was a problem. De Grazia borrowed the $25.00 down-payment for the land from his brother, but funds for building materials were scarce and sporadic.

"It took years to complete," he recalls. "Sometimes I would just say 'The hell with it!' and go off prospecting for gold in the Superstition Mountains." De Grazia's partner on his many prospecting trips was a man named "Shorty" Thorn. De Grazia and Shorty never found their "pot of gold," but this failure was for the most part probably due to Ted's philosophy concerning treasure. "I've always been obsessed with the idea of finding gold," he admits, "but on the other hand, I've always been afraid I might find it."

"Somehow," he mused, "the hunt has always meant more to me than the kill."

He laughed. "You know, I remember how Shorty and I used to try to make money. We tried everything. Once we even tried to make diamonds! That didn't work out too well.

"I had read someplace that carbon made diamonds. I didn't know a damned thing about it, but when Shorty came by one day with a big chunk of ore he said was titanium, I decided to teach Shorty how to make a diamond.

" 'Titanium?' I said. Hell, that's what they make diamonds out of!'

" 'Really?' asked Shorty. 'How do we do that?'

" 'Simple.' I replied. Carbon and hydrogen and oxygen . . . that will give us all the temperature we need. We'll just put it in the kiln, apply the torch, and the son-of-a-bitch sure will make a diamond!'

" 'O.K.' said Shorty, 'Let's do it!'

" 'What we want to do,' I said, 'is keep this thing cooled at the same time we're heating it, and I don't see how we can miss.'

Shorty was impressed.

"We got some guy to help us rig up the kiln with an arrangement of spray nozzles for cooling it, put the carbon and everything in the kiln, lit the torch, and sat back to wait."

Ted laughed.

"We came back in about five hours, and the damned thing was all melted into a mass of nothing. Shorty didn't believe it. He looked heartbroken.

" 'Where's the diamond?' he asked."

PROSPECTOR, oil, 24" × 30"

De Grazia continued.

"In those days, we couldn't make a penny no matter how we tried. I once got a call from a fellow who wanted one of my paintings, and he said he would drop by to see a few. I rushed outside and put some lobster and crab shells around my hammock—so he would be impressed with the fact that I was eating high-class food—then stretched out in the hammock and tried to look bored.

"He wasn't impressed. Turned out he was a grocer, and I wound up trading a 4×8 foot canvas for $18.00 worth of groceries. Funny thing though . . . the grocer got a divorce a few years later, and he cut that painting in half as part of the settlement. He hung his unsigned half of the painting in the front window of a junk shop, and advertised it for $50.00. Some guy who recognized my work drove by one day and saw it, so he slammed on his brakes, went in and bought it. "Recently," he continued, "this same guy sold that one-half of a painting for $1000.00! No one knows what happened to the other half."

Although gold continued to elude the impatient De Grazia, it was during this period of his life that he found a different kind of treasure . . . he met and married his present wife, Marion. "Miss Mary," as he calls her, recalled the experience with a softness in her eye and voice.

"I came to Arizona quite by accident. I was living in the East. I heard of Arizona; its beauty, cactus and Indians. My first stop was Tucson.

"It was a momentous decision for me.

I'll never forget my introduction to De Graz'.

A girl friend took me by his studio. He looked up, stared at me for a moment, and said, 'Where have you been all my life?'

The next week we were married.

"The wedding took place in the jungle of Mexico, somewhere in the Isthmus of Tehuantepec. It was an Indian wedding. We had an old wreck of a car and no money, but it was an experience I will always treasure."

Marion walked to a corner and returned with what looked to be an emerald necklace cast in silver.

"See this? De Graz' knew my birthstone was an emerald, but he couldn't afford any such thing in those days. All he had was a chunk of raw silver ore from one of his mining expeditions; this is the result!"

She held the necklace with the heavy "emerald" pendant up to the light. "It's only a piece of melted 7-Up bottle, cast in silver, but isn't it beautiful?"

There was no other way to describe it. It was beautiful.

Her voice grew softer. "We were very happy in those days."

But the days were not all happy for "Miss Mary."

Ted De Grazia is a man of many moods.

Old Studio

TED De GRAZIA AND HIS WIFE MARION.

He can be sensitive and giving to a fault. At other times, he can emerge from a "brooding" session with an intensity and "demand" for understanding that brings pain to those around him. On occasion, during the early years of his marriage to "Miss Mary," he would disappear into the desert for weeks at a time. "I am afraid," he admits, "that I was not always a good husband. But how could it be otherwise? An artist should never be married in the first place. The price you pay to be an artist is greater than any damn fool who wants to be one can imagine. It comes out of your money, your hide, your soul or your spirit. When a young person comes to me and says, 'De Grazia, I want to be an artist,' I say, 'Don't!'

"No," he continued, "an artist should never be married. You must work alone too much of the time. You can never create anything in a crowd. Your wife will say, 'Don't you love me?' What's that got to do with it? How can you talk in terms of conventional expressions and demands of love when your guts are on fire, and your mind is churning with a thousand things that are trying to get out and *be*?

"An artist must sacrifice too many things; family, security, privacy. . ." He paused.

"You know, privacy is a luxury; you have it because you can afford it. Privacy is like growing a beard—you have one because you can afford it, or because you are a damned fool! Always, we have to give up something for something . . . it's not just choosing what

MARION'S EMERALD

to give up that's hard, but rather choosing the right time. When is the right time? For example, when is the right time to die? The important thing is to do something . . . right or wrong, do something! There's no more miserable way to live than as a 'blank cartridge.'"

For certain, Ted De Grazia is no blank cartridge. Perhaps the most striking feature of De Grazia, aside from his unique talent as an artist, is his boundless energy. Those who know him well declare that they have never known him to take a vacation. Whether painting a work of art, or constructing a building, he approaches the task with dramatic vigor. Through the bold strokes of a palette knife, his paintings erupt in striking color from the canvas; if during the night he were to conceive an addition to his studio, it would not be unusual to find him making the adobe blocks for its structure before morning. Nothing deters him.

"I figure a man can be what he wants. He can't go beyond his experience, but if he works hard enough and—more importantly— lives long enough, he can always reach his own star. I've got what I want. I could make more money if I wanted to bury myself in work and worry. Why should I? I've got all the money I need. Too much money can be vulgar. If you get too big, you lose control of your life. I hate business; it has a way of dictating the way you live and act. I like my way of life because of the challenge, but not for the money. When you're not spending as much as you are taking in, then you are making too much money! Money is not God; at my age, who cares? Money is strange . . . it's like a woman . . . it's wild. You play hell getting it when you go after it, but turn your back and there it is."

But it was not always so. There were many tough years at the Campbell and Prince gallery when De Grazia cared very much. In those days, he found it hard to visualize ever having enough money.

In front of the De Grazia studio, on the Campbell Avenue side, ran an irrigation ditch. Ted put boards across the ditch and covered them with rows of ceramics and assorted pottery. In the center of this array he placed a beautiful hand-cast candelabrum, some three feet high. This work now stands in his home. It is not for sale, but if it were, the price would be prohibitive to all but the most affluent collectors. In those days, it had a price of $25.00!

"It wouldn't sell," recalls De Grazia.

"In fact, I had a time selling anything. One day I got so discouraged I said 'the hell with it!' and got drunk. I forgot my ceramics, and the candelabrum, and left them outside on the ditch all night. In the morning I was even more discouraged. No one even bothered to steal them!"

Finally, things began to pick up. Between 1947 and 1951, De Grazia turned out a prodiguous number of paintings. Between his constant travels into Indian country, sketching, painting, and collecting information for future works, he also found time to visit New York, where he explored possibilities for reproducing paintings in volume on cards and prints. De Grazia laughingly recalled his first "print" experience.

"I wanted in the worst way to see some of my work reproduced in prints, so I worked

34 up my courage and approached an engraver in Southern California. I showed him a few paintings.

I said, 'You know, if you print these, I think I can sell them.'

I didn't know the first damned thing about color separations, or procedure, or cost. I just knew I wanted to see some of my things reproduced.

He said, 'Where you from?'

I told him, and he said, 'How many can you buy?'

"That depends upon how much they cost.'

He said, 'Oh, about a dollar each.'

He was, of course, thinking in terms of doing quantities of a few thousand. I said,

WALKING LADY

'Well, in that case I think I can afford about fifteen!'

The printer thought that was very funny, but he went out on a limb and carried me. Sure enough, I began to sell prints quite successfully. Today, of course, we sell prints by the millions."

By 1951, the picture was definitely beginning to develop a rosy tint. De Grazia sold a few paintings through the efforts of good—and farsighted—friends such as Buck Saunders in Scottsdale, Arizona, and Hiatt's in San Juan Capistrano, California, and he was also doing very well indeed in the card business.

Still, there were problems to be solved. First, galleries still refused to show his material. Second, the population explosion in Tucson began to disturb him.

True to nature, he once more turned to the desert and mountains for breathing room. This time he looked to the north, toward the rocky foothills of the Santa Catalina Mountains. Once more he would build himself a gallery. This time, it would be a Gallery in the Sun!

Prospectors Shorty Thorn and De Grazia, Superstition Mountains

Chapter Five

All things return to dust
Save beauty fashioned well;
The bust
Outlasts the citadel.

THEOPHILE GAUTIER

It is not without reason that De Grazia's Gallery in the Sun is listed among the architectural wonders of Arizona. One may describe the technical aspects of its structure—such things as the hand-wrought iron doors and the "mine tunnel" entrance. It is not too difficult to envision the thick adobe walls, or the ceramic decorations, or even the unique slices of cholla-cactus spine, cut and embedded artistically in one section of the gallery floor. It is impossible, however, to create for even the most perceptive reader, the sense of peace, contentment, and esthetic delight engendered by the beauty with which the whole is fashioned, or the manner in which this beauty almost imperceptibly blends into Nature's desert garden surrounding. In De Grazia's own words: "It is a place for remembering. A place in which to begin to believe."

The first structure of the Gallery in the Sun was literally lost in the desert. De Grazia made his own trail to the new studio. It was the beginning of what is now an explosive growth movement to the north of Tucson. In addition to the new studio, De Grazia also built a little mission in honor of Our Lady of Guadalupe. The roof is open to the sky, ". . . as it should be," affirms De Grazia, "You can't close up God in a stuffy room!" Colorful, religious murals decorate the walls of the Mission, and at one end of the aperture in the center of the roof, a cross of cactus-spine tops the structure as a natural symbol of the surrounding desert.

Today, there are many individual galleries in the complex. The reason has little to do with the desire for growth. The additional galleries have been built by De Grazia to house the growing collection of original work which he refuses to sell.

Visitors to the Gallery in the Sun are often confused by the fact that even though a painting might have a price tag attached, it is usually hanging next to a sign which reads "No paintings for sale!" Confronted with the question, De Grazia replied, "Why should I sell them? I would just have to paint more to keep filling up the gallery." He laughed—"It's always nice to quit when you're on top!"

De Grazia fans are growing increasingly frustrated by their inability to acquire "originals." One lady recently wrote De Grazia a long letter stating that, "Once in awhile one has a great disappointment. . ." She went on to describe how she had attempted to purchase a De Grazia original in the Tucson gallery while Ted was away. She was told, "No paintings for sale," but it was suggested that she try Old Town, San Diego. The next day she traveled to San Diego. She found one place with an original De Grazia, but it was not for sale. She and her husband had been saving for years to buy a De Grazia, and now that they had the money, they could not find

PHOTO BY LOUISE L. SERPA

38

Gallery "Mine Tunnel Entrance"

Gallery In The Sun

PHOTO BY PETER HUTH

one for sale. "Would he please help her?"

De Grazia does have a standing offer for anybody interested in acquiring one of his originals. He will not sell it for money, but he will trade any painting for gold. Some people have actually taken him up on his offer. He was approached by an old friend recently, and handed a Bull Durham sack full of gold nuggets. De Grazia was surprised, but true to his word he laughingly agreed to trade for a small bronze.

As a result of this disinclination to sell, De Grazia originals are becoming more scarce and more expensive. This is offset by the fact that excellent reproductions of his works are available to literally millions of individuals who can scarcely afford a De Grazia original.

Further millions of De Grazia prints have been sold by charitable organizations. As an example, De Grazia donated the use of his "Navajo Madonna" to the American Cancer Society in 1964. A quarter-million cards were sold for over $55,000.00 in the United States alone. Needless to say, De Grazia is today a far cry from the contemporary image of the "poor painter." He accepts his new-found affluence casually.

"People in the art business always want to know, 'How did you make it?' There is no formula for success in an art career. I got in through the back door. I've always spoken my mind. I tell people to go to hell if I don't agree with them. I'm not saying that this is the way to make it, but I will say that if you

PHOTO BY SHERMAN CHUCK

Gallery's West Wing

Preliminary sketch of the new gallery

Gallery's main room off entrance

PHOTOS BY SHERMAN CHUCK

Gallery's south wing with cholla cactus floor

Detail of cholla cactus floor

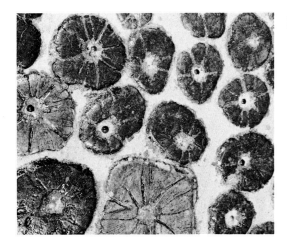

42

"Confessional"
Our Lady of Guadalupe Mission

do make it this way, you will sure as hell enjoy it more!

"And," he continued, "it isn't getting money that counts anyway. Having no money conditions you. You never really change, even when you finally get it. I remember I used to sleep in the car on the side of the road because I didn't have three dollars for a motel room. I ate crackers and sardines instead of a meal in a restaurant. I still have an inclination to turn off the lights in a motel, and take the extra bars of soap for future use.

"You always come back to your basic principles. You may stray away while experimenting with superficial 'kicks,' but you always come back. I used to get a kick out of spending money simply because it was a new experience. I had always dreamed of owning a convertible car. Finally I got one; a bright, new red one. After that, there were many. Now I just want something to take me where I'm going . . . I no longer care about impressing anybody."

By 1952, De Grazia was looking for new fields to conquer. His paintings were selling well, and the Gallery was flourishing, but he wanted something more to satiate his boundless energy. Upon impulse, he accepted the offer of a New York firm to use his talents in designing textiles. Monetarily, it was a successful venture, but De Grazia quickly grew tired of New York. He returned to the deserts of Arizona and immediately

packed off on a prospecting trip to the Superstition Mountains.

During the next few years, De Grazia created great consternation among his friends and followers by his refusal to capitalize on his success—as any reasonable businessman should. In short, he did exactly what he pleased. He described it as his "INGS" period. Prospecting, painting, smoking, drinking, or, he affirms with a wink, ". . .any other damned 'ing' you can think of."

Much of the De Grazia "legend" is built around this elusive period of his life. Stories of his eccentricity are endless.

Preliminary sketch of
OUR LADY OF GUADALUPE Mission

Our Lady of Guadalupe Mission

44

Sahuaro skeleton door

Altar, Our Lady of Guadalupe

"Is it true," asked one critic, "that De Grazia has six wives scattered around the Southwest and Mexico?"

"I don't know about that," answered another, "but you can bet he has twice that many children—legal or otherwise—running around the countryside!" As might be expected, De Grazia will neither confirm nor deny. He merely laughs and changes the subject.

1958 was a turning point in De Grazia's career; Hallmark put his work on Christmas cards, and he began to emerge as a national figure. In 1960, he did a painting for UNICEF entitled "Los Niños," which alone sold over five million boxes of greeting cards. In 1961, NBC came to De Grazia, followed shortly by Hollywood. The result was a documentary about his work, filmed in Mexico.

Although De Grazia is as much at home in Mexico as he is in his own Arizona, seldom will he travel alone. This is not only because he dislikes driving alone, but also because he likes to have a "sounding board" along for his ideas. On occasion, these trips

into Mexico are somewhat harrowing, as was the Hollywood documentary trip in 1961.

As a background to the story, the Director was interested in shooting some footage of the murals on which De Grazia worked with Rivera and Orozco in the early 1940's. This was a John Anderson production, and the Director was Lee Garmes, who filmed *Gone With the Wind*. The Americans were to supervise the proceedings, but they were compelled by contract to hire a Mexican film crew to do the actual shooting. Ted recalled the experience with some humor.

"We stayed in the most expensive hotel in Mexico City. I remember Lee Garmes asked me, 'De Grazia, where did you stay when you were here in 1942?' I pointed to a park across the street. 'Right over there,' I said, 'on that park bench with the rest of the Indians.'

"They wanted to see where I worked with Rivera at the National Palace, so I took them over. We went up to the second floor, past the guards, and I pointed out the sections they wanted to see. I could see the guards were getting suspicious as to what it was all about.

"We then went outside to the *Zócalo*. Across the street there was a little Mexican boy, standing on the steps of the Mexico City Cathedral. 'That's what we want!' they said, 'a shot of De Grazia painting a Mexican 'waif!' "

De Grazia pulled at his beard and a twinkle appeared in his eye. "Hell!" he

BOY WITH SOMBRERO

Gallery patio

laughed, "I didn't even know what a 'waifer' was. Anyway, this Mexican crew set up some reflectors and started shooting film from all angles; they were even lying down in the street. A Mexican policeman came by; then another. Finally a car pulled up, full of policemen. One of them said to the Mexican Director, 'Where's your permit?' It turned out they didn't have one. I was still trying to paint the Mexican boy . . . and, as the 'star,' look unconcerned at the same time. It didn't work. A big cop walked over and pointed his finger at me, 'You are all going to jail?' he said.

" 'O.K. by me,' I replied.

"They drove us to jail and locked us up. Finally they came by and started to ask for identification papers, visas, etc. You might know it, I had lost mine. I decided to pass myself off as a Mexican.

" 'What's your name?' one of them asked me.

" 'De Grazia.'

" 'What else?'

" 'That's all, just De Grazia.'

"The policeman scratched his head and turned to his partner. 'Is that possible? Just one name? He can't have just one name!' The partner shrugged his shoulders. 'Where are you from?' he asked.

'From the North,' I replied. They assumed I meant northern Mexico. Apparently that—and the fact that some five hundred dollars changed hands as a "*mordida*"—

Textile designs

NAVAJO MADONNA, oil, 7" x 12"

48

LOS NIÑOS, oil, 24" × 26"

satisfied the Mexican authorities. They said, 'O.K., you can all go.'

"We were just going out the door when the phone rang. One of the cops answered it, then yelled at us, '*Alto!*'

"We stopped.

"He said, 'Who is the North American painter?'

"'*¿Quien Sabe?*' I replied.

"They let us go, and we went right down and boarded a plane for Acapulco." Ted laughed, "I don't know how or why, but I always seemed to get into trouble more easily when I was younger. Things have been pretty tame lately . . . you think that's because I'm becoming a philosopher?"

If Ted De Grazia is a philosopher, he has an unconventional approach. For certain, he doesn't spend any *idle* time in contemplation. In 1962 he completed the paintings for the book, *Padre Kino,* then built a gallery room to house the collection. This was followed in 1964 by the *Way of the Cross*—again a new gallery room to display the original art for that publication. In 1965

De Grazia was welcomed back to Morenci, Arizona with an elaborate ceremony in his honor. Since then, there have been many books, films, national television appearances, and a growing army of De Grazia fans. It is true that there are those who still reject his work, but there is no question that he is fast becoming a national celebrity. Ted accepts it very casually.

"I'm not impressed with the fact that I'm supposed to be famous. All that really means—once you start to believe it—is that people have some kind of an unnatural 'hold' on your life. I don't want anybody, or any situation, to dictate how I live my life.

"As an example, my insurance man called me some time back and insisted that I carry the same insurance as one of our more famous loud mouth políticos from Arizona."

"'Why?' I asked him.

"'Well,' he said, 'you're a famous person. You have more in assets now. At least, you should let us insure your hands.'

"'I'll tell you what,' I replied, 'I'll save you a lot of worry. You just cancel everything. Cancel all my insurance. You guys have me at the point now that I'm afraid to live and afraid to die!'

"'You're joking!' he said.

"'Like hell I am! I figure I've paid enough taxes to cover the cost of my burial. If I can't afford to pay for my own funeral, then let the county do it.'"

49

CANDLE GIRL

De Grazia is just as casual about people who fail to admire his art. People often walk into his studio, take one look at his paintings—some of which are deceptively simple in appearance—and say, "My kid can do that!"

"That's fine," he replies. "you should put him to work. By the way, has he sold any lately?"

On one occasion, a group of women were bartering for some De Grazia prints. Upon hearing the price, one said, "Why, I can get prints like that for a dime-a-dozen!"

De Grazia pulled a dime out of his pocket.

"That's wonderful!" he said, "bring me a dozen."

Commenting on his own work, De Grazia said, "I never cease to be amazed how few people really understand art. Oh, they may buy it, but I mean to really understand what it is they have bought, or why they bought it. I don't expect everyone to like my art. If it has meaning for them, then it is good for them. If it has no meaning, then they

INDIAN & BABY

shouldn't buy it. I collect the art of painters I admire . . . Picasso, Gauguin, Chagall . . . and I have some by Western artists like Berninghaus and Charlie Russell. I feel I can communicate with these artists, because I think I understand what it is they are trying to say.

"But the thing is," he continued, "you don't have to be a trained and polished artist to have something to say in art. A 'primitive' can say a great deal, even if he doesn't know one damn 'rule' of art." He laughed. "I remember one of my critics used to follow me all over. She told someone, 'I make a point of coming to all of his showings, just to tell him how much I dislike his paintings. He can't call himself a painter; he breaks all the rules!' "

De Grazia continued. "Not to know a rule in art and break it is bad art, but to know a rule and break it is good art. Only by knowing the rules and breaking them will one develop an individual style. Unless, of course," he chuckled, "you happen to be a really natural 'primitive' like Shorty Thorn! Shorty came to me some years back with one of these pictures you paint by number. I sat him

INDIAN WEDDING AND BAPTISM
(Kino Collection) oil, 20" × 15"

51

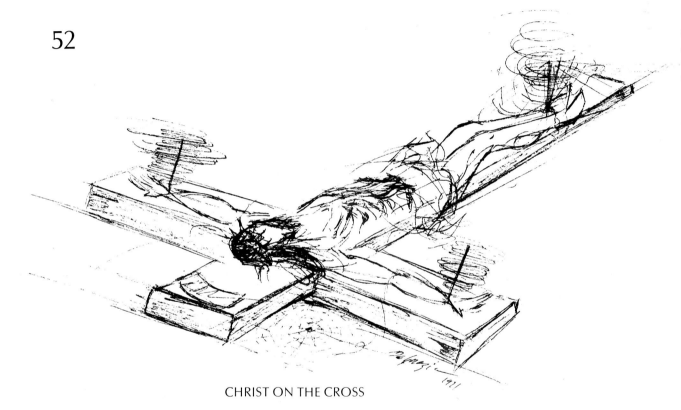

CHRIST ON THE CROSS

down at a canvas, gave him some brushes and colors and told him, 'Now paint!' Sure enough, he painted. He ignored the rules because he didn't know the rules.

"Shorty is a primitive. A man in our civilization can be a primitive. He isn't necessarily a man who can't read or write and has never seen a painting. I'm a primitive in finance, for instance. I don't like bankers. I bury my money."

De Grazia elaborated on the above in a small booklet which he wrote and published in 1965. It was entitled:
Gene Thorn—Painter.

. . . . Shorty hasn't attempted to see other people's work. He picks up his brush and paints . . . and he comes up with pleasant pictures. Since he doesn't know the rules, he can just paint. . . . If Grandma Moses was good, if Henri Rousseau was good, then certainly Shorty is good. . . .

I purposely have not told Shorty about art because this is confusing. People should not read about art. They should go by instinct. . . .

Schools emphasize the wrong things in art. A child will paint and do very well until he goes to school and gets to a certain grade. The teacher will tear down what the child has done. 'There is no such thing as a blue horse,' she will say. 'The proportion too is wrong.'

Most painters, after they get their schooling, wish they could revert to what Shorty Thorn has done. . . .

You can't compare Gene to Michelangelo and Da Vinci. Thorn's painting is like a fine drink. You savor it. You don't analyze it. You view his paintings not as critics, but as people who like charming things.

As a result, Shorty Thorn today has his own studio in Tucson, and is happily engaged in painting the world as he sees it. In a recent conversation with a friend, Thorn commented on his *compadre* of many years, Ted De Grazia:

"Ted and I took a trip to California some years back, and we were in that town . . . you know . . . where the birdies come back?"

"You mean San Juan Capistrano?" asked the friend.

"Yeah!, that's it. Anyway, we was havin' a show there at Hiatt's, and someone asked if I was going to have a show of my own. Ted told the guy that Thorn never would show unless they agreed to let De Grazia show too!"

Shorty laughed. Then with a gruff-softness in his voice, he asked a question, almost to himself.

"Ain't he a hell of a guy?"

Shorty Thorn's question may well be the best answer to the many unanswered questions concerning De Grazia. He has found his "Gallery in the Sun," but it is evident to those who know him well that he has also found—in the honest friendship of people like Shorty Thorn, and in the growing recognition of his contribution as an artist—something which will, indeed, ". . .outlast the citadel."

INDIAN BOY

Chapter Six

A man who has tried to play Mozart, and failed, through that vain effort comes into a position better to understand the man who tried to paint the Sistine Madonna, and did.

GERALD WHITE JOHNSON

The setting was the Colonial Room of a luxury hotel in Tucson, Arizona. Guests in formal attire wandered in boredom from busy group to group, sipping champagne while waiting for the guest of honor. The occasion was a press conference and cocktail party honoring the release that evening in New York of De Grazia television special. A film of the special was standing ready on a projector in the center of the room, and the master of ceremonies had a worried look on his face. "What if De Grazia didn't show up? One never knew . . . he was a bit eccentric you know."

Suddenly, the front door swung open, and all eyes shifted to focus on the reason for their being there. He was a man of medium stature, with an unruly beard and a mischievous twinkle in his eye. He was wearing Levi denims and a Levi jacket with a large tear in one elbow. In stark contrast, his shirt was a pleated "after six" variety, open at the neck and topped with a bright-colored cowboy neckerchief. An Indian medicine bag hung over his shoulder on a strip of rawhide leather. As the television cameras swung in his direction he grinned, held up one hand signalling a pause, and pulled from the bag a pint of whiskey. He took a quick drink from the bottle, wiped the back of one hand across his beard, smiled at the group, and walked forward to his seat of honor. The party was officially commenced.

"Who in the hell is that?," asked one uninitiated guest.

"You mean you don't know?," his friend replied, "That's De Grazia the artist!"

The foregoing is typical of the irreverence with which De Grazia deals with the "sacred cows" of society. Few men are more gentle and understanding of the real needs and sorrows of individual persons. Few people, also, are more critical of fabricated or institutionalized social demands. Like the late H. L. Mencken, De Grazia uses iconoclasm as a constructive tool. "If you puncture someone's sacred balloon," De Grazia commented, "then they feel compelled to defend their position. Good defense takes research, and sometimes a little honest research can lead a person to ask himself a few embarrassing questions about what it is he's trying to defend."

Recently, De Grazia was on his way to a rather stuffy board of directors meeting of a Tucson corporation, when he spied a Yaqui Indian friend on the side of the road, quite

DeGrazia's "Cavalry,"
Superstition Mountains

57

DeGrazia with Yaqui Indian friend

58

YAQUI DEER DANCER
Cast bronze, Height: 10"

obviously in an advanced stage of drunkenness. On impulse, Ted stopped his car and invited the Indian to take a ride. Upon reaching his destination, De Grazia took the Indian upstairs to the oak-paneled corporation office, and introduced him to a quite speechless assemblage as his financial manager.

"It's rather interesting," said De Grazia, "to see how someone handles a situation where the rules don't really count."

Perhaps because of his unique approach to life, perhaps because of the fact that he is simply and uniquely himself, De Grazia exerts a charisma that is fascinating to behold. De Grazia "fan clubs" have sprung up in the past few years in cities and hamlets throughout the Southwest. On the rare occasions when he can be induced to travel beyond the limits of Arizona or Mexico, he is accorded a royal welcome from New York to California. Among his friends, he makes no differentiation based on social status. At any given time, one may find him entertaining national personalities such as Broderick Crawford—who visits De Grazia from time to time to "get in a little painting"—or one of his many Indian friends, in from the reservation with children, parents and grand-parents, to visit "Señor Ted."

A television personality of some fame called De Grazia recently at five o'clock in the afternoon. She announced that she was bringing some of her friends around to see his studio.

"I know you have a log chained across the Gallery entrance after hours," said the actress. "Will we be able to get in?"

"That all depends," said Ted.

"What do you mean?"

"Well, I have a very religious Yaqui Indian who is my gatekeeper. I'll tell you what you do. You just drive up and hold your hands out to him, palms upward."

"What's that all about?," queried the actress.

"It's simple. If you have nail scars in your hands he will let you in. Otherwise, my hours are from ten until four!"

Gomi's Restaurant, in West Los Angeles, is a wonderful place to eat. It is not, however, where one might expect to attend an autograph party; unless, of course, it happened to be a De Grazia autograph party. Not only was the restaurant filled to capacity recently, but so was a large tent hired for the occasion

ONE FOR THE ROAD, oil, 5" × 7"

60

Papago Indian coin designed for special edition of DeGrazia Biography. Limited Edition, 200 copies. "Indiains" mispelled

of De Grazia's premier of two new books and a series of new paintings entitled "De Grazia Paints the Signs of the Zodiac." The tent was placed alongside the restaurant, in the parking area, and for three days a steady flow of De Grazia fans, from politicians to movie stars, from educators to factory workers, braved all obstacles to obtain an autograph or shake hands with Señor De Grazia.

Two days later, De Grazia proved it was no fluke by repeating the performance at Cole's Book Shop in La Jolla, California, and again at the Old Town Gallery in San Diego. Ted took it in stride: "Sure I get tired. After a week of traveling, meeting thousands of people and signing hundreds of books, cards, and prints, anyone would be tired, but that's part of the price you have to pay. They are my public . . . they put me on top. I love them and they love me. Still, the more you are exposed, the less time you have to call your own. That's what I mean when I say I'm fighting overexposure. I need time alone—'brooding' time.

"If I were a 'technician' instead of a creative artist, then there would be no problem. I can't do it that way. I can't really create something unless I have time to live with it for awhile, alone. You can't be an artist unless you know what 'aloneness' means. You don't become an artist by going to school, where they 'sugar coat' you. To become an artist, you start inside and work out. You

must be dedicated, and you'll sweat it out every minute of every day. It's difficult, and there's no guarantee of anything, and you will pay dearly and nobody will know and nobody will care."

Ted pointed to his paintings hanging on the walls of his studio, and piled in stacks in every corner of the room. "That's what it's all about. That's my life-blood hanging there on the wall. I believe that being an artist is one of the most difficult professions in the world; nobody believes you're good until you make it, and you begin to doubt you're good after you make it. By that, I mean you become more and more critical of your own work, and begin to realize that you can never reach the peak of your own expectations because there just isn't enough time.

"I was once asked on a television show to give advice to young art students. I said, '. . .first you must be able to grow a beard, and then you must wait until it turns white!'

De Grazia got a mischievous twinkle in his eye. "Actually, I hate artists. They are miserable bastards! I can count the good ones on one hand. Most of them are just mechanics who have learned their lesson well. After they learned their lesson they adopted—or accepted—some kind of a 'label,' and they have been stagnating ever since.

"Everybody wants to label you. I've been called everything in the book. You would be surprised how many people call me an abstractionist. I am not an abstract artist. I've done it on occasion, but I am not an abstract artist. I do, however, respect it. You can respect something and not like it.

"Actually, I like Medieval art. I like it better than I do Renaissance art. I was thrown out of school once for saying that! I think Medieval artists painted because they wanted to, while too many Renaissance artists painted because they were paid to. That makes a hell of a difference in a man's art.

"As I said before, I think Church art is among the best art in the world, but too often the Pope was up there calling the shots. Nobody, not even the Pope, can tell an artist how to create! That's something you can only do by yourself. Praying may help. Not

that I would pray for help...I never ask Christ for favors; he looks tired to me."

De Grazia is correct when he says that there is no label for him. There could be none. He never stands still long enough. Deceptively simple in appearance, and in his approach to strangers, De Grazia is in actuality a many-faceted personality. Faced with challenge he is a tough opponent. When confronted by the demands of a society which insists upon a mediocre "normality" of behaviorism, he rebels. This has earned him the reputation among some as being an impossible eccentric—a classification which he shrugs off with a tolerant smile. Relieved of the necessity of defense, and secure in the intimacy of his own domain, he is a warm and generous personality who gives unstintingly of his time and talent. More important than the viewpoint of others is the way in which he views himself:

"I don't know what all the fuss is about. De Grazia ain't so hard to understand. You know, when somebody doesn't act and think like everyone else, people want to make him into some kind of a nut. I think that helps them sleep better. Besides, I'm not so damned different. Like most people, I want to do something worthwhile with my life."

Ted turned and called to "Miss Mary."

" 'Marion! Bring your book over here.' "

A few moments later Marion appeared and quietly moved up behind his chair. She gazed down at him for a moment before handing the book over his shoulder, and a fleeting smile broke the usual dignity of her

Marion DeGrazia's MADONNA
Cast bronze, Height: 2½"

WOMEN CRYING WITH 3 CROSSES

features. The soft touch of her hand upon his arm was almost imperceptible, as she turned and as quietly moved away. "Take a look at that!" said De Grazia, as he proferred the book for examination. It was a small booklet containing numerous full color reproductions of striking, free-form bronzes. They were sensitively fashioned and beautiful beyond description. Ted waited for a nod of approval before continuing.

"Those are 'Miss Marys' ' You know, she went to Columbia University?" It was a visible effort for him to conceal his pride. He continued. "Marion and I have an idea. We are going to make the waxes for 100 of our works and seal them in a vault with the stipulation that one piece is to be taken out and cast each year for the next 100 years after we die. That way, if a child is born on the day we die, and if he lives to be a hundred years old, he will be able to see a new De Grazia creation each year of his life! . . . A living museum!"

De Grazia stared at the soft flames dancing in a corner fireplace. After a few moments, he turned and pointed to a row of

The Desert Rest

"Bull Durham" tobacco sacks hanging from a rafter across the room.

"See those? I keep them there to remind me that once a sack of Bull Durham was the only thing I owned in this world. Since then, I have owned many material things, but I've also come to realize that we don't really own anything. We just spend a few years here, and hopefully enjoy a few things along the way. If we are more fortunate, we may even be able to contribute a few."

De Grazia glanced toward the door behind which "Miss Mary" had disappeared a few moments earlier. This time, it was the Man who spoke, and not the Artist.

"Up until three or four years ago, I lived in a world of my own. I was impossible to live with. Now, for the first time in my life, I find myself going home to Mama."

He pulled the inevitable red handkerchief from a hip pocket and blew his nose. After a while he looked up and grinned.

"Even an 'irreverent angel' needs a good companion!"

PHOTO BY MARY ALLISON THATCHER

PHOTO BY LOUISE L. SERPA

65

The many faces of De Grazia

Reproductions by Category of the
major works of Ted De Grazia

DESERT MEDICINE MAN, 24" × 36"

TRAILS END, 24" × 44"

BUTTERFLIES, 16" × 10"

A LITTLE PRAYER, 20" × 14"

70   *A BEAUTIFUL BURDEN, 5" × 7"*

LITTLE PAPOOSE, 10″ × 7″

71

72

NAVAJO GROOM, 24″ × 9″

NAVAJO BRIDE, 24″ × 9″

APACHE GUIDE, 18" × 28"

RED BULL, 6" × 8"

PICADOR, *24″ × 18″*

75

76 CLASSICAL NATURAL, *16" × 12"*

PADRE KINO BRINGS CATTLE
TO THE ALTAR VALLEY 1687
(Kino Collection) 24″ × 36″

TWO SQUAWS, 7″ x 10″

78 *MY FRISKY HORSE, 7" × 5"*

STAMPEDE, 24" × 36"

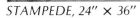

DONKEY, 10" × 12"

FLOWER BOY, 12" × 9"

FLOWER GIRL, 12" × 9"

HANUKAH, 20″ × 14″

JESUS STRIPPED OF HIS GARMENTS
(Way of the Cross Collection) 20" × 15"

84

MOUSE
5" × 4"

EAGLE DANCERS, 24″ × 18″

HOPE, 20″ × 14″

86

SCORPIO
16″ × 12″

SAGITTARIUS
16″ × 12″

87

MUD HOUSE AND INDIANS, 6" × 10"

RED BOWL, 10" × 7"

FLOWERS FOR ALL, 21" × 13"

89

90

INDIAN LULLABY
16" × 12"

COCHITI PUEBLO DANCER
16″ × 10″

DEVIL DANCERS
24″ × 18″

BALLET DANCER
20" × 14"

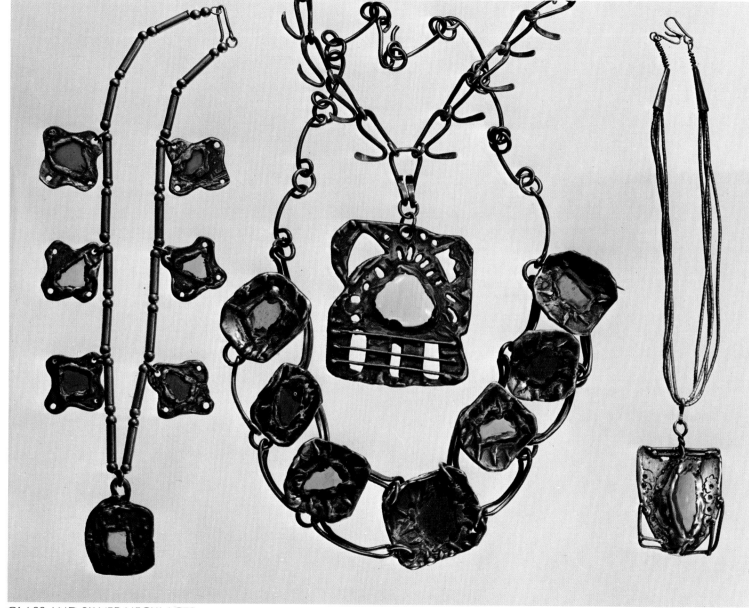

GLASS AND SILVER NECKLACES

SILVER CROSS, Length 3"
Silver Fused to Glass

HO-HO-KAM BELT, silver

*SERI INDIAN
AND SEAHORSE*
Height 3"
Original wax cast in silver

SILVER MADONNA, Height 8"
Original wax cast in silver

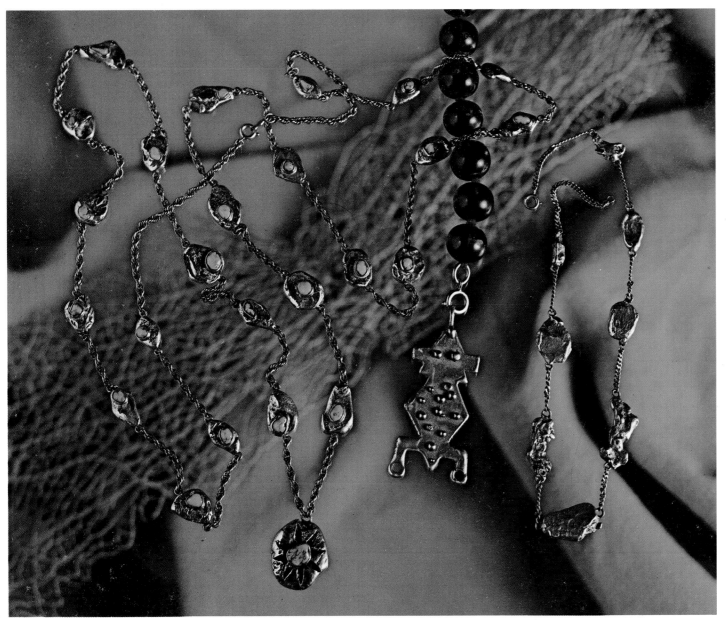

GOLD NUGGET NECKLACE

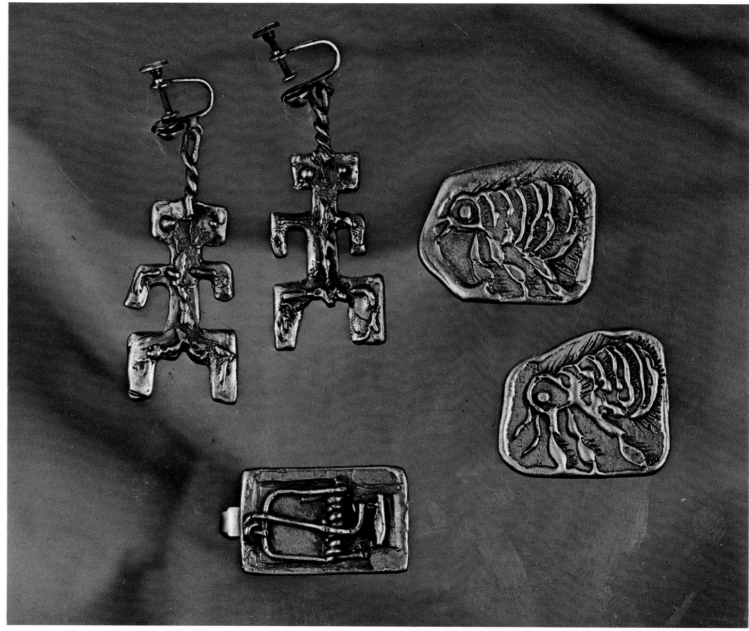

PICTOGRAPH, earrings, FLEA, cufflinks, silver, MOUSE TRAP, tie clip

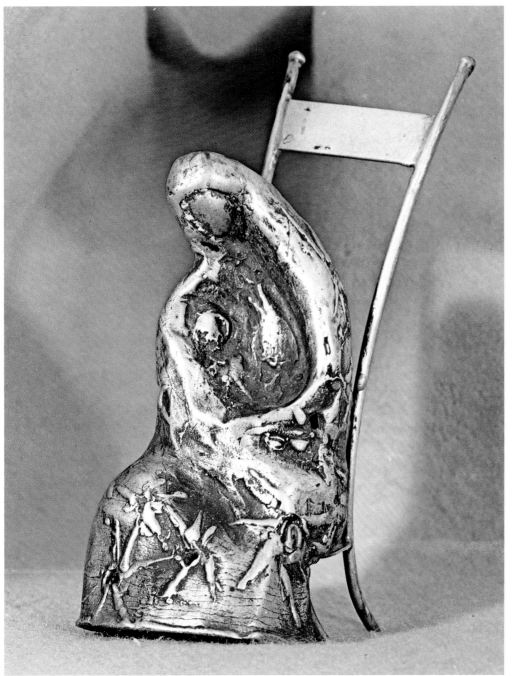

MADONNA AND CHILD, silver, 5"

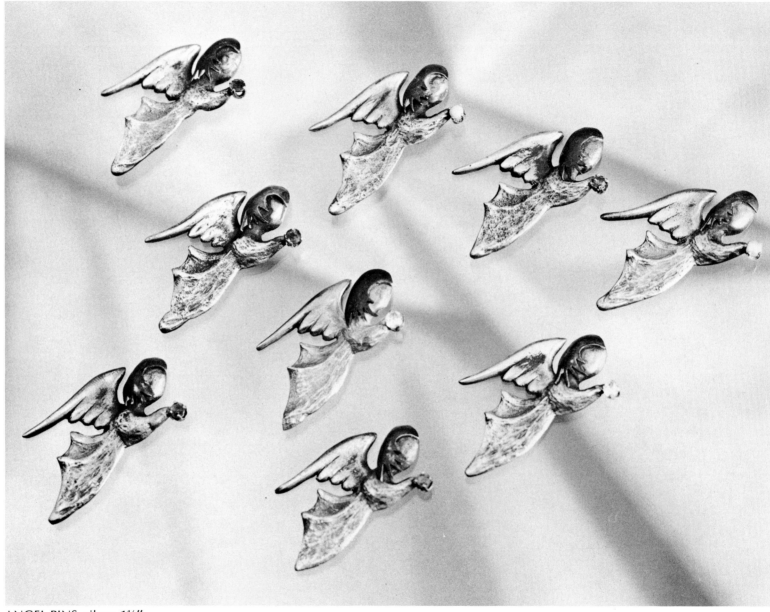

ANGEL PINS, silver, 1½″

Platter: CAVE DRAWINGS, 17"

102

THREE WOMEN, 8"
Shell ceramic

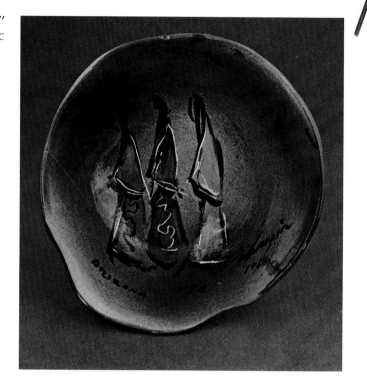

ST. FRANCIS IN TILE, 22"

ROOSTER, 11"
Natural desert clay

103

104

SAHUARO PLANTER, 5½"
Cast from Sahuaro tip

CACTUS PLANTER, 12½"
Cast from barrel cactus

105

CHARIOT HORSE, 17"

ETRUSCAN HORSE, 17"

108

LITTLE BLUE HORSE, Length 7"

CROSSES, ceramic painted with turquoise, Large 14", Small 8"

BLUE MADONNA, Tile, 8"   109

110 ONE MERRY-GO-ROUND HORSE,
Ceramic horse set in silver, Height 7"

APACHE DEVIL DANCER,
Height: 22½" Cast in clay

112

COMEDY AND TRAGEDY
*Cast ceramic masks, 4",
and silver earrings, 1"*

CANDELABRUM, Height: 24"
Original ceramic, inspired by the
jungles of Mexico

114

FAWN, 5½"
Tile mold

QUAIL, 5½"
Tile mold

115

Cameos
116

Yaqui: TAMBOLERO

FIVE WOMEN ASCENDING, 16″ × 8″
Inspired by Dante's Inferno
Plaster modeled with a brush

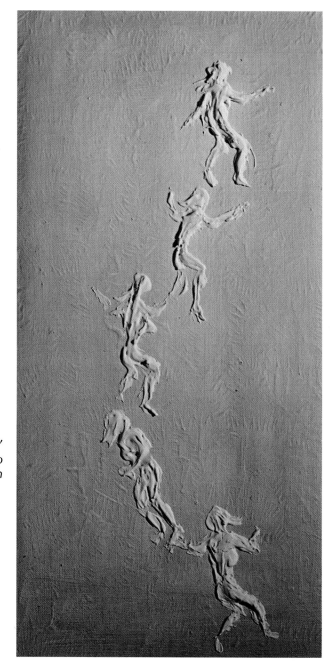

Serigraph
117

THREE NAVAJOS, 16″ x 20″

Encaustics
118

THE CHRISTENING, 10" x 8"

PINK CHRIST CRUCIFIX, 9¾" x 8"

THREE FIGURES PRAYING, 15¼" x 11¾"

Oils on Wood

120

THEY STAND AND WAIT, 10" x 5¾"

WISHING, 6″ x 6″

121

122

THE ANGEL'S HORSE, 9" x 6"

FLOWERS FOR ALL, 17" x 6"

BOY WITH A BASKET, 20″ x 16″

Pastels
123

124   A BEAUTIFUL BURDEN, 20" x 16"

Bronzes

126

THE DANCING FRIARS, (FRS. Serra, Crespi, Palou) Height: 6" Cast bronze

FATHER KINO, Height 7½", Cast bronze

INDIAN HORSE, Height 3", Cast bronze

HO-HO-KAM FLUTE PLAYER,
Height 10" Sand cast in bronze

MERRY-GO-ROUND, cast bronze, height 10"

130

ANGEL TURNED MADONNA,
Height 10½", Cast nambe

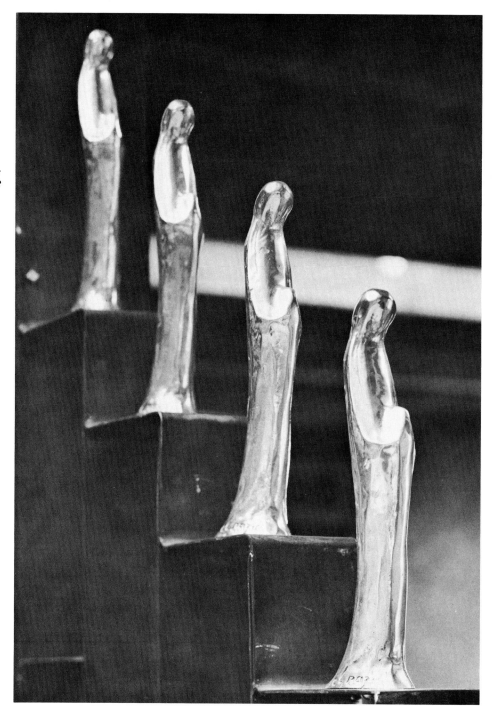

ST. FRANCIS, Height 12", Cast bronze

COYOTE, Length 4½", Cast bronze

LADY OF LOS ANGELES MEDALLION
2¾", Cast bronze

APACHE HUNTER
Height 8", Cast bronze

134

NAVAJO FAMILY, Height 8", Cast bronze

ROAD RUNNER, Length 13½", Cast bronze

136   *THREE PADRES, Height 4", Cast bronze*

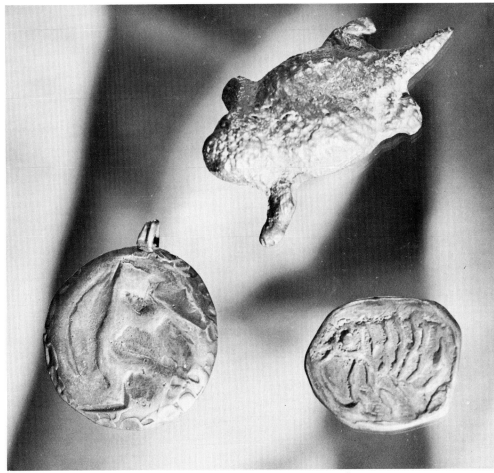

137

HORNED TOAD, Cast bronze, FLUTE PLAYER, FLEA, Cast silver

ANGEL, Height 10½", Cast nambe

138

SOUTHWEST MINING CLUB, cast bronze 3"

ROSE AND THE ROBE, cast bronze, height 5"

MOUNTAIN SPIRIT, Height: 9"
Original in beeswax

140

TIRED PADRE, height 6", beeswax

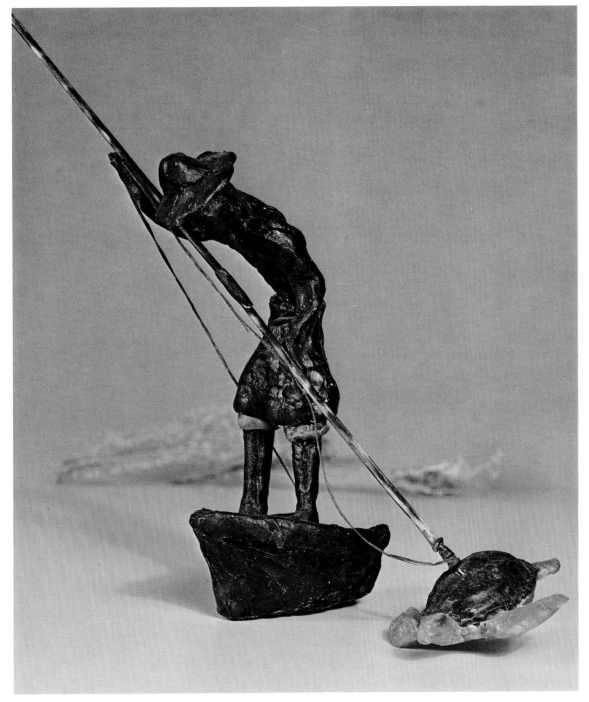

SERI INDIAN HARPOONING TURTLE   141
Height: 7" Original in beeswax

142

SERI ON CEREMONIAL LEATHERBACK TURTLE, Height 3¼″, Original in beeswax

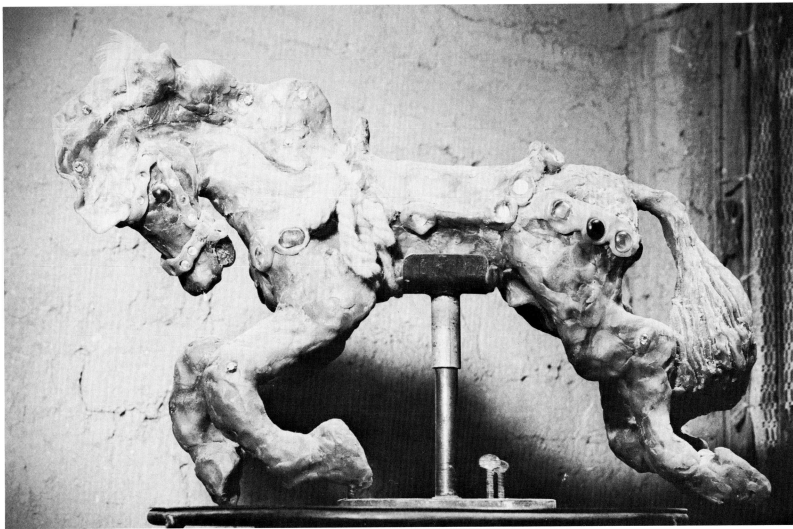

JEWELED MERRY-GO-ROUND HORSE, Length 26½", Original in beeswax

144

CHOLLA CACTUS CANDLE
Height: 9" with cactus base

DANTE'S INFERNO CANDLE
Height 12"

Glass on Glass
146

OUR LADY OF GUADALUPE
8", Glass fused to glass

FOUR WOMEN WALKING, 10" x 8"

Stained Glass
148

SUNFLOWER
Height 15½", Stained glass

EXPECTATION, height 12″

149

Watercolors

150

INDIOS A DONDE VAN 8½″ x 11″

a Beautiful Midnight Sketch
winter 34m of 1971
DeGrazia y
ARIZONA USA

MOTHER AND CHILD 8½″ x 11″

ANGEL ROADRUNNER, 3½" x 5"

MAGIC HORSES, 3½" x 5"

154   INDIOS DEL RIO GRANDE, 8½" x 11"

COWBOYS, 8½″ x 11″

155

156

LUMINARIA FIESTA, 3½" x 5"

MADONNA TAKES A CHILD, 3½″ x 5″

158   SOLDIER, 8½" x 11"

TO EACH IT'S OWN, 8½" x 11"

159

160

CHILDREN, 8½" x 11"

13/20   INDIAN DREAM HORSE   DeGrazia ARIZONA 1971

INDIAN DREAM HORSE, 10" × 8"

162

12/20   TWO PUEBLO INDIANS   degrazia 1971

TWO PUEBLO INDIANS, 4½″ × 6″

Desert Indians Cooking 1/25   Ttffragia arizona 1971

DESERT INDIANS COOKING, 8″ × 10″

164

PAPAGO INDIAN BURIAL, 6" × 9"

Three Dream Horses 1/20   DeGrazia Arizona 1971

THREE DREAM HORSE, 6" × 9"

166   *ANGEL FLOWERS, 10″ × 8″*

11/20 Little HELPER DeGrazia 1971

168

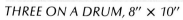

THREE ON A DRUM, 8" × 10"

"Taos Drummer"

TAOS DRUMMER, 10" × 8"

Enamels
170

BOY WITH FLOWER, 8"

BALLOON, 12"

172

APACHE ON HORSE, 3", Enamel on silver

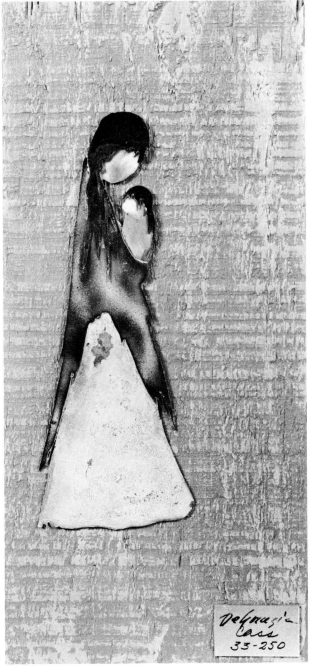

NAVAJO MOTHER, 6" Enamel on copper   *ANGEL AND SAHUARO, 6", Enamel on copper*

174

HORSE, 6" Enamel on copper

CANDLELIGHT PROCESSION, 8¾", Enamel on copper

175

Furniture
176

COFFEE TABLE, mesquite wood, and miner's picks

Coffee table, CAVE DRAWINGS

Miscellaneous

178

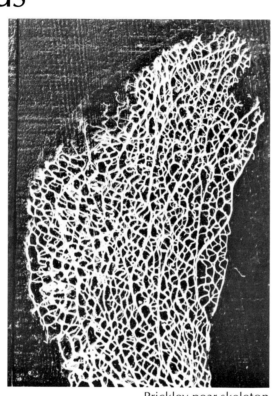

Prickley pear skeleton

Gallery counter, serrated wood tiles

180

HO-HO-KAM DESIGNS,
one of many sources of inspiration
for DeGrazia

182

CHILDREN BEGGING, 4" × 6", Etching on steel

DREAM HORSES, 3½″ × 5″, Etching on steel

184

EASTER EGG, 3½"
Goose egg

ROOSTER WITH MARBLE EYE, 11", Iron

ANGEL MOBILE, 14"

Bibliography

De Grazia's Books, Articles,
Films and Recordings

DE GRAZIA, THE AUTHOR

BOOKS

ah ha Toro. Text and Illustrations by Ted De Grazia. Flagstaff: Northland Press, 1967.

"Art and Its Relation to Music in Music Education." By Ted Etterino De Grazia. Unpublished M.A. thesis, University of Arizona, 1945.

The Blue Lady: A Desert Fantasy of Papago Land. Book 5 of Arizona South. Tucson: De Grazia Studios, 1957.

De Grazia: Illustrated Catalog of Reproductions. Tucson: De Grazia Studios, 1961-1970 Vols 1—This was an annual catalog. The title varied.

De Grazia Paints the Signs of the Zodiac. The author's limited proof edition with personal comments. Tucson: De Grazia Gallery in the Sun, 1971.

De Grazia Paints the Yaqui Easter; Forty Days of Lent in Forty Paintings with a Personal Commentary. Tucson: University of Arizona Press, 1968.

The Flute Player: A Fantasy with dances inspired by Pottery of Ancient Indians Called Hohokam Indians of around Arizona South. Book 2 of Arizona South. Tucson: De Grazia Studios, 1952.

Impressions of Papago and Yaqui Indians. Indians of Southern Arizona. Book 1 of Arizona South. Tucson: De Grazia Studios, 1950.

Mission in the Santa Catalinas: A Tale of Apache Indians, Mexicans and a Mission in Arizona South. Book 3 of Arizona South. Tucson: De Grazia Studios, 1951.

"Padre Kino." A Portfolio Depicting Memorable Events in the Life and Times of the Heroic and Immortal Priest-Colonizer. By Ettore T. De Grazia. Tucson: Arizona South, 1966. This is a folio twenty-two and a half inches by eighteen and a half inches containing twenty separate prints. The only text is a brief introductory note by Raymond Carlson and three short comments as follows: "De Grazia—the Artist, an Evaluation" by Carl Schaefer Dentzel, "Master of Fantasy" by Thomas Hart Benton, and "My Friend, Ted De Grazia" by Ross Santee.

Padre Nuestro. A strange Story of Now and Long Ago. Book 4 of Arizona South. Tucson: De Grazia Studios, 1953.

The Rose and the Robe; the Travels of Fray Junipero Serra in California. Paintings and Text by De Grazia, Foreword by Carl S. Dentzel. Palm Desert, California: Best-West Publications, 1968. This book was designed by John Anderson and printed by Northland Press in Flagstaff, Arizona.

The Seri Indians. A Primitive People of Tiburón Island in the Gulf of California. Ted De Grazia with William Neil Smith. Flagstaff, Arizona: Northland Press, 1970.

The Way of the Cross. Preface by Robert L. Graff. Tucson: De Grazia Associates, 1964. These are reproductions of the fifteen paintings in St. Thomas More Chapel, The Newman Catholic Student Center, The University of Arizona, Tucson, Arizona.

ARTICLES

"Arizona South," by Ted De Grazia. Sketches, Paintings and Water Colors by the Author. *Arizona Highways,* Nov., 1957. pp. 14-25.

"The Blue Lady," by Ted De Grazia whose painting "Desert Madonna" appears on this month's cover. *Desert,* Dec., 1961. pp. 4-5.

"Papago Pilgrimage," by Ted De Grazia. Sketches by the Author. *Arizona Highways,* Oct., 1959. pp. 10-13.

"Texture," by De Grazia. *Mountain States Architecture,* March, 1966. pp. 10-11.

DE GRAZIA, THE ILLUSTRATOR

BOOKS

Benton, Patricia
   The Young Corn Rises. With Illustrations by Itori De Grazia. New York: Vantage Press, 1953.
   "Adaptations of Indian chants, myths and legends."

Brandes, Ray, ed.
   Troopers West. Military and Indian Affairs on the American Frontier. Illustrated by De Grazia. San Diego: Frontier Heritage Press, 1970.

188 Burke, John Patrick

The Picacho Peak Affair. Written and Directed by John P. Burke. Illustrated by Ted De Grazia. Presented by the Arizona Civil War Centennial Commission, Picacho Peak, Arizona, April 15, 1962.
Tucson: 1962.
This is the program of a pageant presented in commemoration of Arizona's participation in the Civil War. De Grazia also designed the stage settings.

Clark, LaVerne Harrell

They Sang for Horses. The Impact of the Horse on Navajo and Apache Folklore. Illustrations by De Grazia. Tucson: The University of Arizona Press, 1966.

Feague, Mildred H.

The Little Indian and the Angel. Illustrated by De Grazia. Chicago: Children's Press, 1970.

Gordon, Alvin J.

Brooms of Mexico. Illustrated by Ted De Grazia. Palm Desert, California: Best-West Publications, 1965.

Gordon, Alvin J.

Inherit the Earth; Stories from Mexican Ranch Life. Drawings by De Grazia. Tucson: University of Arizona Press, 1963.

Gordon, Alvin J.

Journeys with Saint Francis of Assisi. Art by Ted De Grazia. Palm Desert, California: Best-West Publications, 1966.

Paylore, Patricia P.

Kino, a Commemoration. A Short Assessment. Kino Sketches, Ted De Grazia. Bibliography Donald M. Powell. Tucson: Arizona Pioneers' Historical Society, 1961.

ARTICLES

Brophy, Frank Cullen

"San Ignacio del Babacomari." Color by Josef Muench. Illustrations by Ted De Grazia. *Arizona Highways,* Sept., 1966, pp. 2-17.

Candelario, John S.

"Comidas Mejicanas. Exploring the Delights of Southwest Cookery with Author-Photographer John S. Candelario." Sketches by De Grazia. *Arizona Highways,* Oct., 1965, pp. 32-38.

Dobie, J. Frank

"The Road Runner in Fact and Folklore." *Arizona Highways,* May, 1958, pp. 2-11.
Sketch: Ted De Grazia pp. 2-3.

Dobie, J. Frank

"Three Apache Women and a Lone White Man." Drawings by Ted De Grazia. *Arizona Highways,* Sept., 1957, pp. 8-11.

Evans, Edna Hoffman

"The Mysterious Lady in Blue." Drawings by Ted De Grazia. *Arizona Highways,* Sept., 1959, pp. 32-35.

Francis, Marilyn

"Thunder in the Superstitions." Sketches by Ted De Grazia. *Arizona Highways,* Jan., 1965, pp. 2-5 and 44-46.

Heald, Weldon F.

"Tucson, Arizona." *Arizona Highways,* March, 1965, pp. 10-15, 18-32 and 34.
Sketch by Ted De Grazia, p. 12.

Herbert, Charles W.

"Papago Saguaro Harvest." Photography by *Western Ways.* Drawings by Ted De Grazia. *Arizona Highways,* Jan., 1969, pp. 2-7.

Lee, Katie

"Songs the Cowboys Taught Me." Sketches by Ted De Grazia. *Arizona Highways,* Feb., 1960, pp. 34-40.

Norris, Natalie, Editor

"Thru the Old Pueblo with Ettore De Grazia." Vol. 1 of *Follow Me!* 1964—Tucson, 1964.
This was a small guide to points of local interest. It is no longer published.

Peterson, Willis

"El Paisano. The Story of the Storied Roadrunner." Drawings by De Grazia. *Arizona Highways, Aug., 1964, pp. 1-4.*

Richardson, Gladwell
"A Drink for the Dead." Drawings by De Grazia. *Arizona Highways*, June, 1963, pp. 34-39.

Trejo, Arnulfo D.
"The Street Vendors of My Childhood Days." Sketches by Ted Grazia. *Arizona Highways*, Aug., 1963, pp. 36-41.

"A Visit to Mexico's West Coast along the New Highway from Nogales to Guadalajara." Sketches and Water Colors by Ted De Grazia. *Arizona Highways*, Oct., 1955, pp. 3-31.

"Yaqui Easter Ceremonial. A unique, devout, primitive and exciting portrayal of the Easter story that is older than the Oberammergau Passion Play." Text by Dr. Edward H. Spicer, Phyllis Balestrero, and Ted De Grazia. Photographs by Charles W. Herbert, Peter Balestrero, and Sherman Chuck. Illustrations by Ted De Grazia. From the book "De Grazia Paints the Yaqui Easter." *Arizona Highways*, March, 1971, pp. 2-11, 34-35 and 45-47.

Arizona Days and Ways Magazine. The Arizona Republic, April 3, 1966. Front page "Holy Week" by De Grazia.

Illustrations and sketches by De Grazia are scattered throughout the issues of the following:
Arizona Highways

March, 1961	December, 1964
December, 1961	February, 1968
July, 1962	December, 1969
November, 1964	December, 1970

National Wool Grower, April, 1971
Front cover by De Grazia.

Orange County Illustrated, Jan., 1969.
Front cover by De Grazia.
This magazine is published in Newport Beach, California.

"This Week in Astrology" prepared by Carl Payne Tobey for Newspaper Enterprise Association, Inc.
This weekly column which is published in twenty-four newspapers was illustrated in 1969 by De Grazia.

WAK Facts, Dec., 1965. Illustrations throughout the entire issue by Ted De Grazia.
WAK Facts is published by the Labor Management Committees of the W. A. Krueger Co., Brookfield, Wisconsin. Their business is lithographic printing.

Butler, Ron
"Mission in the Sun." *Avenue,* January, 1969, pp. 66-72. *Avenue* is published in Amsterdam, The Netherlands. Except for the title the article is in Dutch.

Cahill, Mary
"On the Eve of Fiesta." By Mary Cahill. *Sandal Prints,* Nov.-Dec., 1965, pp. 26-30.
The full title of this publication is *Sandal Prints in the Capuchin Missions.* It is published by Capuchins in Detroit.

Carlson, Raymond
"An Artist in Navajo Land." Illustrations by Ted De Grazia. *Arizona Highways,* Aug., 1967, pp. 14-29. Also front cover.

"Christmas on the Desert." *Arizona Days and Ways,* Dec. 22, 1963, pp. 10-15.

Conrotto, Eugene L.
"One Man's Southwest, the Story of Tucson Artist Ted De Grazia." *Desert,* Dec., 1960, pp. 22-25. Also front and back covers.

Cutts, Anson B.
"De Grazia." *Point West,* Aug., 1960, pp. 18-21.

Davis, Loda Mae
"De Grazia—Arizona's Impetuous Impasto." *The Trumpeteer,* Spring Edition, 1952. Unpaged.
The Trumpeteer was published in San Francisco.

De Grazia, Marion
De Grazia; a Biographical Sketch. Tucson: Gallery in the Sun Publications, 1966.
This small book compiled by Mrs. De Grazia includes four pages of "Midnight Sketches" in pen and ink, a one page "Chronology," a two page summary of De Grazia's life, nine pages of color reproductions of pictures he has done "to help others," and six pages of photographs of the artist and his friends.

"De Grazia." *Arizona Highways,* March, 1949, pp. 28-35.

"De Grazia Painter and Potter." *The Magazine Tucson,* Oct., 1948, pp. 30-31.

190 "De Grazia Shows Master's Form." *The Arizonian*, Oct. 20, 1967.

"Eramaassa on Elamaa" (There is Life in the Desert). *Eeva*, Tammikuu, (January), 1968, pp. 46-47.
This magazine is published in Helsinki, Finland.

Feague, Mildred H.
"A Red Handkerchief in His Hip Pocket." The Mildred Feague-Ted De Grazia Story. Prescott, Arizona: Mildred H. Feague, 1970.
This is a six page pamphlet with a picture and a sketch.

Keatley, Vivien
"Mission in the Sun." *Arizona Highways*, Nov. 1955, pp. 30-37.

Kew, George
De Grazia in Chiaroscuro, Photographic Studies. Tucson: Photocenter, c. 1963.

Los Angeles. Southwest Museum.
Padre Kino: Memorable Events in the Life and Times of the Immortal Priest-Colonizer of the Southwest Depicted in Drawings by De Grazia: with Commentaries on the Artist and His Work by Noted Authorities on Southwestern History and Art. Los Angeles: The Museum, 1962.
This is a quarto size, black and white edition of the folio listed under De Grazia, The Author. In addition to the pictures, the contents are:
Introduction by Carl Schaefer Dentzel.
Padre Nuestro. A Strange Story of Now and Long Ago by Ted De Grazia.
Ted De Grazia, Master of Fantasy by Thomas Hart Benton. Kino-De Grazia, An Historical Perspective by Raymond Carlson. De Grazia the Artist. An Evaluation by Carl Schaefer Dentzel.
My Friend, Ted De Grazia by Ross Santee.

McClure, Clara
"Ted De Grazia—Artist with a Mission." Photos by Bill Beebe. *Outlook West* in *Evening Outlook*, May 16, 1970. Cover and three unnumbered pages. Santa Monica, California: United Western Newspapers, Inc.

Maw, Dolly
"Artist-Genius, Hermit-Millionaire De Grazia." *San Diego Magazine*, Dec., 1968, pp. 90-93.
Also front cover.

"Mission in the Hills." *Western Ways*, April, 1954, pp. 14-17.
Also front cover.

Nelson, Kitty Jo.
"Poet with a Palette." *Arizona Days and Ways*, Sept., 24, 1961, pp. 24-25.

"Notes from the Editor." *Arizona Living*, April, 1963, p. 4. Describes a weekend with Ted and Marion De Grazia.

"Painting Music in Color. Untaught Artist Seeks the Relation between Art and Music." *Pix*, April, 1948, pp. 12-13. *Pix* is published by Associated Newspapers, Ltd., Sydney, Australia.

"The Power of Positive Space." *Architectural Record*, Dec., 1957, pp. 172-173.

Shaw, Elizabeth
"Painter's Pilgrimage." Paintings by Ted De Grazia. *New Mexico Magazine*, Jan., 1965, pp. 24-27 +.
Also front cover.

Shaw, Elizabeth
"Ted De Grazia." *Phoenix Point West*, June, 1964, pp. 36-40.

Southern Arizona Chapter of the American Institute of Architects. Buildings of Architectural Significance in Tucson. Tucson: 1960. De Grazia's Mission in the Sun is one of the nine buildings described in this little folder.

"Southwestern Sheen." *Counterpoint, The Magazine of Music and Allied Arts*, June, 1952, p. 27.

"Sun of Originality." *The Trumpeteer*, July, 1950, pp. 38-39.

"Ted De Grazia. The People Painter." *Arizona AAA Highroads*, November/December, 1970, pp. 4-5 +.
Highroads is the official publication of the Arizona Automobile Association.

Corrida. Tucson: Gallery in the Sun.
> Written and directed by Mark Clark. Photography and editing by Alex Hankocy.
> Twenty-three paintings of the bullfight. Color, sound, 16 mm. Time: 10 minutes.

De Grazia. Tucson: University of Arizona Radio-TV Bureau. Film Department, 1967.
> Written and produced by Stephen Kearns. Photography and editing by Harry Atwood. Narrated by Robert Hayworth and Ted De Grazia. Music by Carlos Mogro, guitar.
> This production was made possible by the National Endowment of the Arts. It won a Golden Eagle Award by CINE in Washington, D.C. in 1968. It is in color and with sound and runs for 29 minutes.

The Rose and the Robe. Tucson: The Gallery in the Sun.
> Written by Terry Thure. Photography and editing by Alex Hankocy. Original music by Richard A. Heatly. Voice of Father Serra by Robert W. Keyworth.
> The paintings from the book of the same title. Color, sound, 16 mm. Time: 22 minutes.

The Way of the Cross. Tucson: Gallery in the Sun.
> Written and directed by the Rev. Robert L. Grass. Photography and editing by Harry Atwood.
> The paintings of the fifteen stations of the cross in the Newman Catholic Student Center of the University of Arizona. Color, sound. Time: 12 minutes.

"Brooms of Mexico." Lyric by Alvin Gordon. Music by Larry Shayne. On Verso:

"Fiesta at De Grazia's." Alvin Gordon, Ted De Grazia, Robert McBride, Gregory Millar, Travis Edmonson. Accompanist: Los Principés.
> Tucson: Travis Enterprises, Inc.
> De Grazia did the art work on the envelope of this record.
> He also joins in the conversation on the "Fiesta" side.

"Tortillas." Book and Record. Story "Tortillas" by Alvin Gordon. Music and Narration by Travis Edmonson. Art by Ted De Grazia.
> Tucson: Travis Inc., 1970.

"Viva California." An Early California Pastorela for Orchestra and Chorus. Performed by the Elizabeth Waldo Folklorico Orchestra and the St. Charles Choir.
> 350 Years of California Musical Tradition of the Indian, Spanish and Mexican Periods Accompanied by a Descriptive Text and Beautifully Illustrated by Ted De Grazia.
> Los Angeles: Southern Music Publishing Co., Inc., c. 1969.

The author wishes to acknowledge a debt of gratitude to the many persons whose unselfish assistance and guidance made this book possible. A special thanks to Alice W. Wilson, for permission to use the appended bibliography of De Grazia's works.